Outer Banks Cuisine
A Sampling of Our Restaurants
With
Recipes

by Becky Smith

Becky Smith

Outer Banks Cuisine
A Sampling of Our Restaurants
With Recipes

Dirt Enterprises
Printed 2014
All rights reserved
Copyright © 1999-2013

Published by; Becky Smith
Dirt Enterprises
P.O. Box 262
Harbinger, N.C. 27941

Web site: www.chefdirt.com
E-mail: beckysmithobx@yahoo.com

Cover Design: Becky Smith

ISBN: 978-0-9662656-7-5

Printed in the United States by Morris Publishing®
3212 East Highway 30
Kearney, NE 68847
1-800-650-7888

Outer Banks Restaurants

Aqua Restaurant & Spa
Avenue Waterfront Grille
Awful Arthurs's Oyster Bar
Back Porch Restaurant
Bad Bean Baja Grill
Bambino's
Barefoot Bernie's
Basnight's Lone Cedar Café
Beachside Bistro
Big Al's Soda Fountain & Grill
Black Pelican Oceanfront Café
Blue Moon Beach Grill
Blue Point, The
Brewing Station
Brine & Bottle, The
Café Atlantic
Café Franko
Café Pamlico
Capi'n Franks
Chilli Peppers Restaurant
Colington Café
Darrell's Restaurant
Diamond Shoals Rest. & Seafood Mkt.
Dirty Dick's Crab House
Duck Deli
Dunes Restaurant, The
Elizabeth's Café & Winery
1587 Restaurant
Fishbones Raw Bar & Restaurant
Fishbones Sunset Grille & Raw Bar
Fish House Restaurant
Flying Fish Café
Full Moon Café, The
Good Life Gourmet Rest, The

Goombay's Grill & Raw Bar
Great American Grill, The
Grits Grill
Henry's Beef & Seafood
High Cotton
Howard's Pub & Raw Bar
Hurricane Mo's
JK's Restaurant
Jason's Restaurant
Jolly Roger Pub & Marina
Jolly Roger Restaurant
Kelly's Restaurant & Tavern
Kill Devil Grill
Kimball's Kitchen
Life Saving Station
Lucky 12
Mako Mike's
Metropolis Martini Tapas Bar
Mike Dianna's Grill Room
Miller's Seafood & Steak House
Miller's Waterfront Rest.
Mulligan's Raw Bar & Grille
North Banks Restaurant
Ocean Boulevard
Orange Blossom Café
Ortega's
Owen's Restaurant
Pamlico Jack's
Peppercorn's Restaurant
Pier House Restaurant
Poor Richard's Sandwich shop
Port O' Call Restaurant
Red Sky Café

Outer Banks Restaurants

Roadside Raw Bar & Grill
Route 12, Steak & Seafood
Rundown Café
Sam & Omie's
Stripers Bar & Grill
Sugar Creek Restaurant
Tale of the Whale
Top Dog Café
Tortugas Lie Shellfish Bar & Grill
Trio
Vilai Thai Kitchen
Weeping Radish Farm Market & Brewery

Introduction

Covering 391 square miles of land and 800 square miles of water, North Carolina's Outer Banks (Barrier Islands) stretch from the northern most beaches of Corolla to Ocracoke Island. The Outer Banks long lay in a state of isolation but have undergone a radical transformation in natural character since first sighted by early European explorers. In the days of early settlers the Banks were covered with dense forests as settlers cut the trees to build their homes and boats, the sand was no longer held in place by vegetation. The winds and storms began to move the sand, killing the trees, thus the process continued until the 1930s. The Civilian Conservation Corps then erected sand fences and planted trees and grass on the Outer Banks for stabilization of the dunes.

There were no bridges from the mainland until 1931 and paved roads did not extend the full length of the islands until the early 1950s. Even today, areas north of Corolla can only be reached by traveling on the beach.

The original descendents of many Outer Banks families were shipwrecked mariners that were washed up on the shores of these islands. Many of these men were of English decent. Today, an Elizabethan accent continues to survive on the Outer Banks. High tide is pronounced "hoi toide" and fried seafood is "froid" seafood. History abounds on these stretches of barrier islands.

With so many interesting things to do and places to visit and the wide array of eating establishments to choose from, vacationers will have a hard time deciding what to do first. A handful of tiny fishing villages, miles of pristine beaches, and some of the country's most significant historic sites are located here. The Cape Hatteras National Seashore stretches for 75 miles along the Atlantic Ocean and is the largest undeveloped coastline along the East Coast. Here you will find the famous Cape Hatteras Lighthouse (built in 1870) that stands 208 feet tall, the black and white striped lighthouse is the tallest brick lighthouse in the United States. In 1999, the historic lighthouse had to be moved inward 2,900 feet due to the encroaching ocean less than 120 feet from its base. The journey took 23 days. On November 13, 1999 the Cape Hatteras Lighthouse once again resumed her duty of flashing nighttime warning of dangerous waters. The relocation of the lighthouse has been called "the move of the century" and is an engineering feat that has fascinated millions.

Roanoke Island—Fort Raleigh National Historic Site— the site of the first English settlement in North America should be on your list of places to visit. The Lost Colony outdoor drama tells "History's greatest mystery" of the brave colony of English pioneers of 1587 who encountered natives of a strange new ~world but later vanished without a trace.

Seafood is probably one of the biggest draws for the Outer Banks. Offshore fishing and sound fishing by the local watermen offers a variety of fish such as dolphin, wahoo, tuna, king mackerel, shrimp, oysters, and many others. Many of the local restaurants buy their fresh seafood locally.

The Outer Banks has a wide array of restaurants from which to choose, offering every type of food to please every palate and prices to suit everyone's wallet. Restaurateurs open around early March, April and are increasingly staying open longer into the fall each year. The off-seasons have become very popular for dining out because of the same great food and friendly service with a lot less crowds to deal with. There are upscale cafes with European ambiance and restaurants with extraordinary culinary creations and some with just plain good food.

I hope you will enjoy this book and some of the culinary secrets of the award winning restaurants as a guide to some of the best restaurants on the Outer Banks with special recipes from their chefs.

Vicki Wallace 98

Cape Hatteras Lighthouse
Buxton, NC

Wright Brothers Remembered
First Flight Centennial 1903-2003

Over a hundred years ago, the Outer Banks were no more than sand dunes and wide open spaces, a stretch of barrier islands beside the Atlantic Ocean. Maritime forest and marsh lands were located along the sound. Roads were no more than sand tracks in what was called Kitty Hawk Village.

Wilbur Wright had been invited by William Tate, the Kitty Hawk postmaster, to come to Kitty Hawk to conduct his flying machine experiments. In those days, Mr. Tate ran the post office from his home. The village was then in Currituck county. It wasn't until 1920 that the state legislature moved county lines and made Kitty Hawk a part of Dare County. The Wright Brothers chose Kitty Hawk because the location offered the right conditions for flying. The sand afforded soft terrain for bumpy landings, ocean breezes buoyed the wood frame flying machine, and the dunes provided the elevation for take-off. It was exactly what Wilbur and Orville Wright needed for conducting their gliding experiments.

Wilbur arrived on the Outer Banks in late fall of 1900 to begin his flying experiments. Their first flights weren't successful but they kept at it. On December 17, 1903 at 10:35 a.m., Orville Wright's first flight took place lasting only 12 seconds and traveling 120 feet. Orville and Wilbur made three more flights that day, one of those flights traveled over 852 feet.

Over the years, I had visited the Wright Brothers National Memorial, situated today in Kill Devil Hills. But the historic occasion of the first powered flight centenary made a greater impression on me than I could have ever imagined.

I bought tickets like a lot of people and planned to attend the final event. For no reason, I decided I would go the opening day. Arriving the first day for the event was exciting; I never dreamed that so much could take place on this thin stretch of land, in those few days.

As a little girl, I remember running through the fields, chasing the powered airplanes that flew high above me. That fond memory, and others of flying, came flooding back during that historic week. I hope you enjoy this special edition of my cookbook which is dedicated to the memory of flight, and the brave, determined, and inspired Wright Brothers whose legacy makes air travel possible. "Make the impossible possible." The dream lives on…enjoy

The 1903 Wright Flyer reproduction shown as it was taken back into the building after the re-creation of the Wright Brothers historic flight on December 17, 2003. The attempted re-creation flight failed due to weather conditions, and nearby buildings obstructing wind currents. Those shown left to right are Scott Crossfield, first man to fly twice the speed of sound in an X-15 plane. He was in charge of all flight training for the re-enactment of the centennial flight. Also shown are Kevin Kochersberger, pilot of the Wright Flyer and Terry Queijo, pilots shown wearing 1903 attire.

The Bodie Island Lighthouse

The 170 foot tall Bodie Island Lighthouse was constructed in 1872 on its present site but was the third in a series of lighthouses constructed to supplement the existing Cape Hatteras Lighthouse. In 2010 renovation of the lighthouse was necessary and scaffolding was put in place but hit a snag when significant structural issues were found. A new company was hired in 2012 and by April 18, 2013 the Bodie Island Lighthouse once again officially opened with the original Fresnel lens installed and its tower ready for climbing.

Aqua Restaurant & Spa

1174 Duck Road
Duck, North Carolina
aquaobx.com

Lynette Sumner, Owner,   252-261-9700
John Hester, Executive Chef   Daniel Faircloth, Sous Chef

Perched high on a dune with unbelievable views of the Currituck Sound, Aqua Restaurant has established itself as one of the finer establishments in the Duck area. The soundfront dining room offers spectacular views from every angle. Elegant table settings, seductive sunsets make this restaurant a favorite dining destination. For a more casual dining experience, enjoy a cocktail with friends on the waterfront deck.

Only the freshest seafood, local vegetables, fresh herbs are used in preparation of their healthy menu selections. Entrees include seafood, pasta, prime cuts of meats, pork and fresh salads. Fresh rolled sushi is available Wednesday thru Saturday evenings from 5-10 p.m. Highly recommended is the low country shrimp pasta with NC shrimp, italian sausage, corn, tomatoes, braised kale tossed with penne, plus a delicate shrimp sauce. Also excellent is the line caught NC mahi mahi with israeli cous cous, brussels sprouts plus pancetta, grilled pineapple sauce.

A large bar occupies one corner of the restaurant offering an extensive global wine list, full ABC license. Aqua's mixologist prepares fantastic martinis that you just have to try. Aqua has its own spa offering the latest spa treatments. This restaurant is a great place to have a memorable wedding and reception. A childs menu is available for the little peeps. Open for lunch and dinner in season. Call for winter hours.

Summer music series starts in May and continues throughout the summer on the deck.

Low Country Boil Recipe

(Serves 10-12, Prep time: 30 minutes, Cooking time: 30 Minutes)

Ingredients:

Old Bay Seasoning
5 lbs NC Blue Crab cut in halves
5 lbs Fresh NC Shrimp peeled and deveined
10 ears fresh corn with husk and silk removed
3 packs cooked andouille sausage (cut into 1 inch pieces)
Yesterday's newspaper
Ice cold beer of choice

Directions:

Heat a large pot of water over an outdoor cooker or indoors on stove at medium-high heat. Season the water to taste with the Old Bay and bring to a boil. Add potatoes and sausage and cook for 10 minutes. Add crab and corn & cook for another 5 minutes. Add the shrimp last and cook for another 3 minutes. Put your friends to work! Have them spread the newspaper over the picnic table and fetch the ice cold beers. Low country boil should be fun for everyone. Drain the water and set the pot of goodness on the table for all to enjoy!

Avenue Waterfront Grille

207 Queen Elizabeth Avenue, The Waterfront Shops
Manteo, North Carolina

Thomas & Marie Williamson, Owners,   252-473-4800

Thomas Williamson, Executive Chef

Dine on the historic waterfront overlooking Shallowbag Bay and the state ship, Elizabeth II. View the many boats and yachts that line the waterfront daily. Watch Kayaks glide through the waters while you dine and people strolling the boardwalk. The interior of this restaurant is simple and new with definitely a touch of class.

Avenue Waterfront Grille has a casual, relaxing atmosphere and serves up the freshest seasonal foods. The owners take great pride in sourcing all of their food locally when possible. They are able to take advantage of the growing season locally by offering what is available with changes in menu to showcase fresh ingredients of the day.

The lunch menu offers delicious sandwiches, salads, soup, shrimp and grits and pastas. Dinner entrees include softshell crabs in season, pan seared tuna with crispy rice cake, ginger shitake mushroom cream sauce and bok choy. Also equal to any occasion is the pasta carbonara with chicken or shrimp with linguini pasta, crispy bacon, caramelized onions and creamy parmesan.

The full liquor bar and lounge is a great place to meet and greet friends or that special someone. Marie hand picks all the local beer and wines to reflect their menu.

Open daily for lunch and dinner in season. Call for winter hours. Full ABC license.

Spicy Remoulade Sauce

Ingredients:

1 cup mayonnaise	1 Tbls. Capers chopped
2 tsp. chopped garlic	1 Tbls. Cornichons (crisp tart pickles) chopped
1 Tbls. Whole grain mustard	Pinch of cayenne pepper (to taste)
2 Tbls. Lemon juice	Salt and pepper to taste
2 Tbls. chopped parsley	

Mix all ingredients together and store in a container with a tight fitting lid. Refrigerate.

Awful Arthur's

2106 N. Virginia Dare Trail MP 6
Kill Devil Hills, North Carolina
Jo Whitehead, Owner   (252) 441-5955
Kenny McLean, Chef

A favorite local and tourist spot across from the Avalon Pier,
Arthur's is always busy no matter the time of year. Known as the
"Home of the Happy Oyster", this raw bar promises a good time
and great food. Awful Arthur's is a very casual place where
seafood is the specialty. A large menu featuring everything from
soups and salads, scallops, lobster, oysters, clams, burgers, a
backfin burger · with backfin crabmeat, and sandwiches are
available. Look for the daily entrée specials posted on the large
board. Coastal Living Magazine rated Awful Arthur's as one of
the top ten oyster bars in the nation.

Enjoy the beautiful ocean views while you sip your favorite
beverage along with an appetizers or special of the night in the
upstairs lounge. Several varieties of beer or on tap and a full line of
liquor and specialty drinks are available. Nights are always
extremely busy. Don't forget to pick up one of Awful Arthur's
famous T-shirts. Open year-round for lunch and dinner. Family
friendly, kids menu available.

Awful Arthur's Crab Au Gratin

1 lb. lump crabmeat, picked through
2 lb. backfin crabmeat, picked through
1 pt. heavy cream
½ cup white wine, (preferably the wine served with the meal)
1 T. roasted garlic pepper
2 cups parmesan cheese, grated
4 cups cheddar/jack blend cheeses, shredded
   paprika as needed

Method

1. Mix all together carefully and divide evenly into 8 individual gratin dishes, or large casserole dish
2. Sprinkle with paprika
3. Bake at 350 degrees for 20-25 minutes or until golden and bubbling.

Note: You could use any blend of various crabmeats, seasonings, or cheeses to create a slightly different dish each time it is prepared. A simple yet delicious and satisfying dish...Serves 8

She Crab-Lobster Bisque

4 oz. butter, unsalted
1 large onion, roughly chopped
1 medium carrot, peeled, roughly chopped
1 clove garlic, minced
1 ½ T. paprika
½ T. Awful Arthur's Crab Spice or Old Bay
2/3 cup all-purpose flour
1 qt. clam juice
1 tsp. Tabasco sauce
1 T. Worcestershire

1 pt. heavy cream
black pepper, freshly cracked, to taste
6 oz. backfin crabmeat, picked through
4 oz. Lobster meat, cleaned, and diced
1 oz. dry sherry

Method

1. Melt the butter and sauté the onions, carrots, and garlic until tender.
2. Add the paprika and Awful Arthur's Crab Spice and cook for 1 minute.
3. Add the flour to make a roux and cook 1-2 minutes, stirring constantly
4. Add the clam juice, Tabasco, Worcestershire, and heavy cream, whisking well to incorporate the roux. Bring to a boil and turn off the heat
5. Puree in batches in a blender and season to taste with the black pepper
6. Add the crabmeat, lobster and sherry, and mix well
7. Serve with freshly chopped parsley

Yield: 8 each 8 oz. bowls

The Back Porch Restaurant and Wine Bar

1324 Country Rd.
Ocracoke Island, North Carolina

Daphne Bennink, Owner

(252) 928-6401

Lisa Landrum, Wine Specialist

The Back Porch Restaurant offers some of the island's finest cuisine. Screen porch dining in an elegant atmosphere or eating in one of the small nooks or large open dining room will surely complete a memorable evening on this picturesque island.

The menu features fresh vegetables, herbs, and local caught seafood. All breads, sauces, and desserts are made fresh in the Back Porch kitchen daily. The crab cakes with sweet red pepper sauce are outstanding as is the bourbon pecan chicken breast rolled in pecans, with a bourbon butter sauce. Other recommendations include the Back Porch seafood platter with fish, shrimp, scallops and a deep fried crab beignet. In addition to the outstanding entrees, you won't want to miss trying the crab beignets or one of the restaurants most popular appetizers, Back Porch asiago terrine served with toast rounds. Leave room for some of their fabulous homemade desserts. New to this restaurant is the addition of a wine bar with a large selection of wines and beers. All of their wines are available for retail sale.

It's well worth the trip including the ferry ride, just to eat at this great restaurant. Dinner is served nightly seven days a week. Carry out available.

Back Porch Asiago Terrine

1 lb. Asiago cheese, grated
1 lb. cream cheese
1/3 cup best quality mayonnaise
2 T. roasted garlic, minced or pureed
3/4 cup chopped fresh basil
1 1/3 cup sun dried tomatoes, soaked and chopped coarse
1 teaspoon pepper

Cream cheeses and mayonnaise together, add the rest of the ingredients until blended. Serve warm with toasted walnuts. Terrine can also be served at room temperature as a spread.

Bad Bean Baja Grill

Seagate North Shopping Center
3105 N. Croatan Hwy. M.P. 5
Kill Devil Hills, North Carolina
(252) 261-1300

Bad Bean Taqueria

785 Sunset Blvd.
Timbuck II Shopping Center
Corolla, North Carolina
(252) 453-4380

www.badbeanOBX.com

Rob Robinson, Owner, Chef
Ralf Lang, Chef

Matt Payne, Chef

The Bad Bean Baja Grill offers authentic Mexican cuisine that is anything but ordinary and an atmosphere that sizzles. It's far from your typical Mexican restaurant with flavors adapted from different regions. Bad Bean is the kind of place folks always remember when they return home from vacation. It's also the kind of place local's return to again and again.

Chef Robinson is one of the top classically trained chefs in the U.S. Robinson's cuisine has been recognized by the Washington Post, Food and Wine Magazine, Sante and Culinary Trends magazines. He also was invited to the James Beard House to prepare dinner in March 2005. In 2010 Coastal Living Magazine featured his Fish Tacos.

Chef Robinson opened his first restaurant "The Bad Bean Taqueria" in Corolla in 2005 to rave reviews by tourist and locals alike and recently opened his new restaurant in the newly renovated second location in Kill Devil Hills, tucked away in the corner of the Seagate North shopping center. Airy and bright, the interior of this fun and casual eatery is decorated with scenic murals by Ben Morris, colorful walls and a large terra cotta bar.

Specialties here are the house smoked and chipotle BBQ glazed grilled bone-in pork chop served with chili salt french fries and fresh coleslaw. Another favorite, "shrimp & grits", their take on the traditional fresh local North Carolina grilled shrimp served with monterey cheese and chorizo grit cake toasted on the grill with red chili enchilada sauce and fresh slaw. Everyone loves the fish tacos, choice of mahi mahi or fresh shrimp, served on a toasted flour tortilla with jicama slaw and salsa fresco. For a special treat, try the giant Cali burritos, a meal in a tortilla, filled with your choice of meats, spiced rice, black beans, sour cream, and salsa, all to be eaten like a sandwich. The Bad Bean Brunch is a must try.

A full bar selection is offered serving homemade margaritas (best on the beach) and sangria, Mexican, imported and domestic beers and mixed drinks. Open year round but closed in January. Live music in summer months. No reservations required. There's also a menu for the "Little Amigo."

Fire Roasted Tomatillo & Poblano Pepper Salsa

Ingredients:
20 to 25 fresh tomatillos with husk removed
4 Poblano peppers
1-2 jalapeno peppers, to taste
3-4 Tbls. Canola oil
1 white onion, chopped
4 cloves fresh garlic, minced
1 tsp. coriander
2 cups water
2 bunches fresh cilantro, washed and coarsely chopped

Directions:
Pre-heat grill or broiler. If using broiler, line a cookie sheet with aluminum foil. Place the peppers and tomatillos in a large bowl, and toss with canola oil to coat lightly. Sprinkle with salt. Toast the tomatillos and peppers on all sides until well darkened all over. If using broiler, reserve the liquid released from the tomatillos and peppers.

When cool, pulse in a blender, leaving the mixture somewhat chunky. Add 2 tablespoons canola oil to a large, heavy bottom pot and heat over medium heat. Add onions and garlic, sauté until onions are translucent leaving them with some texture. Add the coriander and cook for only 10 -20 *seconds*. Immediately add the tomatillo and pepper puree and the 2 cups water. Bring mixture to a boil, reduce to a simmer and cook for about 10 minutes.

Fold in the cilantro and season with salt as needed. Cool the salsa immediately. Mixture will thicken as it sits in the refrigerator.

Bambino's

106 Corolla Light Town Center
Corolla, North Carolina
(252) 453-4004

Matthew Broughton, Owner

Located at the northern end of Corolla but within sight of the Currituck Lighthouse is an Italian –American restaurant that is both refreshing and family friendly. This new restaurant occupies the same space that Nicoletta's once occupied. Bambino's menu includes seafood, chicken, pastas, veal, appetizers and salads. Nightly dinner specials along with a host of impressive entrees are sure to please. The main focus here is on local seafood and fresh vegetables.

The main attraction is the cuisine that the owner refers to as Italian-American. Family styled platters are offered. Look for the list of daily specials. Classic dishes using local ingredients are served along with fresh breads made daily.

The wine list here is affordable. The restaurant is family friendly and dress is casual. The owner has recently extensively remodeled the former restaurant and added a full bar. A few seats have been added outside from which to enjoy lunch or dinner. There's a special menu just for the little ones.

Veal Marsala

4 T. Olive oil	salt & pepper
1 pound veal (thin)	1 cup Marsala
1/2 cup flour	butter
mushroom slices	

Heat oil on medium in skillet. Dip veal in flour and coat on both sides. Make sure oil is hot. Fry the veal for *one half* minute on each side. Transfer the veal to a warm platter. Season with salt and pepper and add the Marsala, mushrooms, to the skillet. Boil for a few minutes, add the butter. When sauce thickens turn, the heat down, add the veal, turn veal in skillet basting with sauce once. Transfer veal to a warm platter. Serve immediately over risotto.

Barefoot Bernie's
Tropical Grill & Bar
3730 N. Croatan Hwy. MP 4 1/2
Kitty Hawk, North Carolina
www.barefootbernies.com

Chris Ulabos and Heather Smith, Owners   252-261-1008

Hats off to this tropical grill and bar, they have managed to bring together a touch of class, a tropical island theme with an art deco look blended with great food dishes from some of Chris and Heathers visits to some of the world's finest beaches. This is a great place to meet with friends after a fun day at the beach. Barefoot Bernie's is definitely a local and tourist favorite.

Upon entering this restaurant, the first thing you notice is the huge cherry-wood bar that seems to wrap around one side of the room, surrounded by high top bar tables and six TV's. The open beamed ceilings, paddle fans and tropical posters give a feeling of being in the tropics. This part of the restaurant is for more casual dining or just having a cocktail or glass of wine, while the other side is for much quieter dining with subdued lighting. This restaurant was formerly owned by Chris's family and was know as "Kitty Hawk Pizza" from 1983 till 1999. Pizzas and subs are still part of the menu today.

It's possible to find Caribbean crab cakes, sashimi, coconut shrimp, Cuban style steak and Dominican lime steak kabobs all under one roof. Try salt and pepper calamari or delicious Maryland crab dip for starters. Definitely you'll want to try the "New England clam chowder" which placed 2nd in the 2006 Outer Banks Chowder Cookoff. Move on to more Barefoot Bernie's entrees including the tropical chicken chop with blackened chicken breast over black beans, rice and tomato salsa, or try the, grouper in a bag, with chopped vegetables baked in a parchment bag. This restaurant has something for everyone from appetizers to sandwiches, soups, subs, salads, seafood, steaks, pastas, gourmet pizzas; all made fresh and a special sushi night throughout the year. Desserts are made fresh daily, so make sure you try a favorite.

Open for lunch and dinner year round. Full ABC license with drink specials daily. Entertainment nightly after 10 P.M. in season. Bring the whole family. Child's menu available.

Macadamia Crusted Mahi Mahi with Mango-Corn Salsa

6 oz. skinless Mahi Mahi fillets
1 cup Macadamia nuts, chopped fine
¼ cup all purpose flour

Mix nuts with flour and place evenly on a flat surface (preferably a large plate). Lightly spray one side of Mahi with cooking spray and place on top of nut mixture, lightly press down to make sure nuts stick. Repeat same technique on other side of fish. Preheat oven to 350 degrees. In a small sauté pan preheat 1-2 tablespoons of olive oil. Place Mahi in pan about 1-2 minutes on each side just to toast the nuts. Remove from pan and place fish on cooking sheet and back for an additional 10-12 minutes. Plate Mahi and top with Mango-Corn Salsa. Enjoy!

Mango-Corn Salsa

1 whole Mango, peeled and diced
2 pieces green onion, chopped
1 red pepper seeded, chopped
1 piece yellow corn, cut off the cob
1 tsp. lime juice
1 tsp. curly parsley, washed, drained, chopped
1 jalapeno pepper, seeded, stemmed, diced

Basnight's Lone Cedar Cafe

Nags Head/Manteo Causeway
Nags Head, North Carolina

Marc Basnight, Owner   (252) 441-5405
Bud Gruninger, Executive Chef

May 1, 2007 was a day that left many memories in those that had dined in this wonderful restaurant. Word spread quickly of a devastating fire that had leveled the restaurant to the ground and took with it all of the old fishing memorabilia, duck decoys, and hunting items reminiscent of the old Lone Cedar Hunt Club of bygone era for which this eatery was named. Some wondered if the restaurant would ever be built back, but by some miracle this restaurant opened its doors just months later in time for the summer 2007 season to everyone's amazement.

Every since the Lone Cedar Café opened its doors in 1996, it's been a favorite for tourist and locals alike. Incredible views of the Roanoke Sound can be seen from every table in this casual, upscale eatery. Diners will welcome the change with a much larger restaurant, more seating added to the dining areas and the extended bar area. The restaurant is somewhat similar in design as before but without all the tongue-and-groove walls and ceilings.

This café specializes in regional eastern North Carolina foods using only local fresh vegetables and seafood bought only from local docks. Appetizers, salads, soups, sandwiches seafood and other specials of the day are served for lunch. For dinner try one of the seafood dishes or the prime rib, or pastas, or one of the great nightly specials. One of my favorites is the fried seafood combination with shrimp, scallops, fresh fish, soft shell crab or jumbo crab cake and oysters (in season). There's also a broiled version of the seafood combination. Each day's catch is cleaned and prepared right at the restaurant, so you know you're getting fresh seafood. Save room for some great homemade desserts made from scratch everyday by the resident pastry chef.

Don't be surprised when greeted at your table by Marc Basnight, President Pro-Tem of the North Carolina Senate. He's loves to stop and chat with restaurant customers.

Sausage & Shrimp Pasta

2   oz. extra virgin olive oil
3   T. chopped fresh garlic
½   lb. cooked hot Italian sausage, sliced
1 ½ lbs. jumbo shrimp, peeled and
        deveined (green tails)
4   oz. mushrooms (shiitake, portabella, button)
2   Roma tomatoes, diced
2   bunches scallions, diced
2   oz. white wine (dry)
2   oz. chicken stock
2   T. butter
Grated black pepper
1 ½ lbs. angel hair pasta
Romano cheese

In large sauté pan, heat olive oil. Add garlic, sausage, shrimp and mushrooms and sauté 2 minutes. Add tomatoes and scallions and sauté 1 minute. Add wine, chicken stock, pepper and butter, and simmer 2 minutes. Serve over pasta and top with Romano cheese. Serves 4.

Beachside Bistro

1731 North Virginia Dare Trail, (Sea Ranch Resort))
MP-7 Kill Devil Hills, North Carolina

Restaurant (252) 255-1063   Resort (252) 441-7126

John Romm, Executive Chef   Kathy Gallop, Supervisor
Kendall Byrd, Manager   Rebokah Paul, Bartender

Welcome to Beachside Bistro, the only true oceanfront family dining restaurant on the entire Outer Banks. You'll find this great restaurant inside of the Historic Sea Ranch Hotel. The décor is cosmopolitan chic, casual; with french doors leading into the dining area and beyond, a wall of windows with breathtaking ocean views await. The restaurant has an outdoor patio for casual dining, bordered by sea oats and the ocean just steps away.

Beachside Bistro is everything you'd expect a great family focused restaurant to be with something for everyone, discriminating moms and dads who know good food; to their kids and cheeseburgers. Menu is contemporary casual and prices are very reasonable with many of the lunch choices available for dinner at lunch prices. Be sure and checkout the daily specials and fresh catch of the day on the chalkboard. Executive Chef John Romm is a master of his craft on the Outer Banks offering creative twists to familiar foods using fresh local ingredients. Meals are prepared from scratch daily.

First of all I have to rave about the appetizers; such as the Carolina BBQ eggrolls made with Carolina BBQ and shredded cabbage with slaw jus. I could make a meal out of eggrolls and the hand breaded mozzarella served with balsamic tomato relish. If you love sweet potatoes then you have got to try the sweet potato fries. They are the greatest along with the hand cut french fries. Lunch and dinner menu items include a variety of salads, sandwiches, burgers, fresh seafood, beachside plates and Sea Ranch specialties including steaks. The jumbo lump crab cakes are the greatest along with the plump fried oysters. The desserts are made fresh and are outstanding.

Open for breakfast, lunch, dinner in season serving a breakfast buffet, and Sundays offering brunch. Childrens menu available with milkshakes for kids. Full ABC license. Bar seating.

Jambalaya (Pot Pie)

Ingredients

2Andouille sausage links	2T butter
2T flour	2C milk
3T Cajun seasoning	1C diced chicken (cooked)
3 drops liquid smoke	.5C yellow onion (small dice)
.5C red pepper (small dice)	1.25T minced garlic
.75C raw shrimp chopped	1.5C cooked rice
6 buttermilk biscuits (halved)	

Directions (6 Servings)

1) Cut Andouille Sausage into half moons. Cook sausage, shrimp and vegetables in soup pot, hold.

2) In small sauce pan melt butter and whisk in flour. Add milk slowly and keep whisking as to avoid lumps. Reduce the heat to a slow simmer and add Cajun spice. Stir often

3) Add to soup pot then fold in rice, chicken and liquid smoke. Simmer for 5 minutes.

4) Portion in soup bowls and top with heated buttermilk biscuits.

Bistro Meatloaf

Approximately 10 servings

Ingredients

1 yellow onions small diced	.75t pepper
1.5 carrots small diced	.25t dried thyme
1 jalapeno seeded and small diced	3T minced garlic
1/2C ketchup	1.5T fresh parsley
3.5# 80/20 ground beef	.75C chopped cooked bacon
2.5 cups bread crumbs	4 eggs lightly beaten
.5 T kosher salt	1 T Worcestershire sauce

Glaze

.25C ketchup	2 t. sugar
.25C balsamic vinegar	whisk together and set aside

Directions

1) Sweat the carrots, onions, and jalapeno pepper until translucent, add garlic and continue for 1 minute. Remove from heat and cool.

2) whisk eggs, salt, pepper, herbs, Worcestershire sauce, and ketchup until well blended.

3) Combine beef, bread crumbs, bacon, and cooled vegetables in large mixing bowl. Mix by hand gently, then add egg mixture and mix until all is incorporated.

4) Place in pre-oiled loaf pan and bake at 400 for 45 minutes. Brush on glaze. Cook until internal temperature of 150 degrees, about 15 additional minutes.

5) Let rest for 10 minutes before slicing. Serve in thick slices with additional tomato-balsamic sauce drizzled across it.

Big Al's
Soda Fountain & Grill
100 Patty Lane (Hwy. 64/264)
Manteo, North Carolina
Diane Croswait and Vanessa Foreman, Owners   (252) 473-5570

No matter what age you are, this is a "must do" while on the Outer Banks. The kids will thank you and so will the rest of your family because this is a place you won't easily forget. The theme here is Coca-Cola and I mean in every shape and form that you could ever possibly imagine. The restaurant was built by Vanessa to house twenty years off Coca-Cola memorabilia collected by her sister Diane. Like the Coca-Cola products covering every wall and every glass case, Big Al's is the real thing.

Step back in time to the '50s and you'll think you are on the set of "Happy Days", with Richie Cunningham and the gang. Black and white tiles with red ones thrown in here and there cover the floor and frame the wooden dance floor area, seemingly just made for shagging. Scarlet panels on the Tiffany-style lampshades sport the Coca-Cola script logo. A neon-lit jukebox jumps with everything from Elvis' "Hound Dog" to the Everly Brothers' and the Platters. Don't be surprised if you get the urge to leap from your seat and hit the dance floor.

The old-timey soda fountain is a favorite seating area with its bright red seats and silver-legged stools. You can get all of your old-fashioned soda fountain treats here from banana splits, malted shakes and sundaes to chocolate cokes.

Big Al's offers a variety of sandwiches, juke box burgers, tossin' & turnin' salads and grilled sandwiches. Fried seafood dinners and blue plate specials such as meatloaf, barbecue, chicken, Delmonico steaks are just a few offered daily for lunch and dinner. Soups, chowders and chili are all made from recipes collected over the years from family members. I tried the chicken and rice soup the day I was there, it disappeared quickly due to the fact that it was so good. If you like home made pimento cheese, then, you're going to love the "Good Golly MS. Molly" sandwich served with french fries. It's the best pimento cheese I've ever eaten. The recipe was given to Emma Cannady, mother of owners, by Mollie Fearing, a well-known lady from Manteo. The seafood served here is fresh with a variety of fish, clams, oysters crabcakes and soft crabs available in season.

Breakfast is served daily from spring till late fall. Big Al's is a family oriented restaurant with a game room and a large gift shop. If it's Cola-Cola memorabilia you're looking for, their gift shop will have it or can get it for you. Lil' boppers are welcomed on the dance floor. Prices are reasonable. Lil' bopper menu available. Open daily year round. There's plenty of parking available in rear of building if the front is filled up.

Pimento Cheese Spread
(Good Golly MS. Molly)

2 ½ lb. Cheddar cheese, shredded
2 ½ lb. Swiss cheese, shredded
1 can pimentos (14 oz.)
1 quart mayonnaise
Onion juice to taste

Mix together well and serve

Note: This recipe serves a large crowd. Divide recipe according to number of people served.

Black Pelican Oceanfront Café

3848 Virginia Dare Trail MP 4
Kitty Hawk, North Carolina
(252) 261-3171

Julia Lee, Owner   Jason Smith, Executive Chef

This is one of the favorite restaurants for locals on the Outer Banks with oceanfront dining and open all year serving lunch and dinner. A new addition was added in 1998 with more oceanfront seating and a deck for dining while enjoying the rhythm of the waves. The ambiance is upbeat and casual here.

Black Pelican Restaurant has a lot of history to tell as this gothic structure was constructed in 1874 and was known as "Station Number Six" for the rescue of stranded crews and passengers from shipwrecks. In 1903, Station number Six served as an active weather bureau and provided information on wind velocity for the famous Wright Brothers experiments and later would be used by the Wright Brothers to telegraph the world of the birth of aviation.

Station Number Six originally was manned by one keeper and a crew of six surfmen whose sole purpose was to rescue those people from the violent storms of the Atlantic but were accompanied by a different kind of warrior of the seas known as "The Black Pelican". The large pelican could be seen during violent storms as it would circle around the shore and catch the eye of the surfmen and then swoop down upon the men to warn of a distressed vessel approaching shore. The bird would guide the men through storms to the sinking ships and survivors. Soon many survivors would tell of the same Black Pelican sailing overhead until help arrived.

The large bar is a great place to gather and try some of the great appetizers and drinks. Try one of the Wood-Fired gourmet pizzas; one of my favorites is the White Seafood or the Aloha. Lunch includes a list of daily specials that are awesome. Sandwiches, salads are also served. The dinner menu offers entrees such as Grilled Salmon topped with lemon dill butter, baked shrimp and crab with beurre blanc sauce, prime rib, Kansas City Strip. All entrees are served with seasonal vegetable, red potatoes, and homemade turkish pita bread. Dinner specials are served nightly. Save room for the desserts, these are to die for. Children's menu is also available. Don't forget to check out the *large gift shop. Be sure and not miss the summer season outside deck parties with live music. Catering services available.*

Coconut Shrimp with Peanut Sauce

1 lb. to 1 ½ lbs. shrimp or 35 large shrimp
Breading:
½ lb. of shredded sweetened coconut   1 Tbsp. of all-purpose flour
¾ lb. of chopped pecans (fine)
Combine till completely mixed.

Sauce:
2 can Coco Lopez
2 cans coconut milk
10 oz. Creamy peanut butter
½ teaspoon red pepper flakes

Egg Wash:
6 whole eggs
1 Tbsp. water
Wisk together till smooth

*Whisk together all ingredients
until smooth then refrigerate*
2 cups of all-purpose flour
Dredge shrimp in flour then dip in egg wash and add to coconut breading, toss shrimp until fully coated. Cook in 350 degree oil 1 to 2 minutes until golden brown.

Blue Moon Beach Grill

4104 S. Virginia Dare Trail MP 13, Surfside Plaza
Nags Head, North Carolina

www.bluemoonbeachgrill.com   (252)261-2583

Scott & Melissa Shields, Owners

Scott Shields, Chef   Melissa Shields, Manager

The Blue Moon has definitely made a name for itself and earned its place on the list of best restaurants of the Outer Banks. Chef Shields opened Blue Moon on February 3, 2009 with the encouragement of his family and friends during the worst recession of our times. It didn't take long for the very small but quaint grill to catch on with the locals and tourist and expand to the adjacent building which the restaurant still occupies.

Chef Scott graduated from Indiana University of Pennsylvania's Culinary Academy then moved to the Outer Banks to become the chef at Owens Restaurant in Nags Head and later a chef at Mulligan's on the beach where he met his future wife, Melissa. Together they spent their next eight years working at the Mill Street Grill in Staunton, Virginia with the dream of owning their own restaurant on the Outer Banks someday. That dream came true in a big way with the opening of Blue Moon. The décor of Blue Moon is just as pleasing as the food with colorful art carefully displayed and concrete painted floors which add charm to the setting.

Chef Shields specializes in southern comfort food with a twist. The portions are generous, and the presentation is impressive. A great beginning to a memorable meal is the spinach & arugula salad with champagne poached pear, candied pecans, house smoked bacon, grilled red onion and a creamy goat cheese scallion vinaigrette. The shrimp and grits served over smoked Gouda and aged cheddar cheese, stone-ground grits is a favorite. Another is the crabcake dinner, made their way. The fish tacos are the best with local fresh fish, seasoned, seared and shredded and served in flour tortillas with pico de gallo, cheese, shredded lettuce, and cilantro citrus cream with black beans and rice. For lunch, try the oyster po'boy or the cheese steak & fries. Another favorite is the chargrilled portobello sandwich, served on toasted ciabatta with arugula and a balsamic reduction, served with fries.

Wine by the glass or bottle along with draft and bottle beer are available. Be sure and check out their bar. Child's menu available. Open daily in season. Call for off-season hours. (I asked for a recipe in 2010 and still waiting for it as of 2013).

The Blue Point

The Waterfront Shops
N.C. Hwy. 12
Duck, North Carolina
goodfoodgoodwine.com (252) 261-8090

Sam McGann, Executive Chef, Owner   John Power, Owner, Manager
Joe Panaras, Sous Chef   Dave McClary, Chef de-Cuisine
Matt Estrada, Sous Chef   Joe Santoro, Pastry Chef
Kevin Sprouse, Sous Chef   Julian Alexander, Pastry Chef

In 1989, John Power and Sam McGann opened the Blue Point in the small quaint village of Duck, North Carolina. It was an immediate success with local home owners and tourist alike looking for a contemporary taste of the Outer Banks. Situated among a cluster of shops along a boardwalk, this "gourmet restaurant" offers an expansive view of the Currituck Sound from every seat in the house. Gone is the 1950s-style diner, in its place a newly renovated "Blue Point" with additional seating, doubling the size of the restaurant to more than 100 seats. The dining area now can accommodate much larger groups than in the past. The glass blocks are gone along with the black and white tile floors, replaced with a more" old beach cottage" theme. The bar area has also been expanded. Look around and you might catch a glimpse of those red bar stools and other memorabilia from the past. Now dinners can enjoy watching their favorite meals being prepared in the open kitchen area. An enclosed large porch overlooks the sound and provides an incredible view of the sunset while waiting to be seated.

The Blue Point has been recognized for their excellence in cuisine by such publications as Gourmet, Bon Apetit, Southern Living, Food Arts and many others. In 1995 and 1996, Wine

Spectator magazine awarded an "Award of Excellence" for their in house wine list. The Blue Point received a 3 Star rating from the Mobil Guide. The reasons for these accolades are simple: The cuisine and amenities are impeccable. The cuisine of award-winning Executive Chef Sam McGann is simply outstanding.

The Blue Point is open year round, serving eclectic cuisine for lunch, dinner. Dinner reservations are highly recommended and can be accepted up to one month in advance. This restaurant is a must-do on the Outer Banks.

Scallops Poached in Olive Oil with Rosemary, Black Olives, Roasted Garlic & Lemon

12 Sea Scallops
8 cloves, Roasted Garlic
1 bunch fresh Rosemary
12 large Kalamata Black Olives
4 wedges, Lemon
½ cup Olive Oil
Salt and Pepper to taste

Clean the scallops of the small muscle and pat dry. In a cast iron skillet over medium heat bring olive oil to 300 degrees. Add scallops, roasted garlic and rosemary.

The technique is to poach, not fry, the scallops, so watch the temperature so as not to cook the scallops too quickly, but allow to simmer for one to two minutes. Then add black olives. Turn scallops; continue to cook one to two minutes longer until scallops are just cooked through. Remove skillet from heat. Add a squeeze of fresh lemon juice. Serves 4

To Plate: place on each dish three scallops, roasted garlic, black olives and a spoonful of the seasoned olive oil. Serve with lemon wedges. Toasted French bread croutons or rosemary foccacia would accompany this plate nicely.

Brewing Station

600 S. Croatan Hwy. M P 8 ½
Kill Devil Hills, North Carolina

Aubrey Davis & Eric Reece, Owners   (252) 449-2739
Pok Choeichom, Executive Chef   Tina Mackenzie, Owner, Pastry chef
Scott Meyer, Brew Master   Karen Davis, Front-of House Manager

It's hard to miss this restaurant as you're driving down highway 158 because the first thing you see is the Silo and the tall wind turbine by the highway and you wonder "What's a Silo and a Wind Turbine doing on the Outer Banks. Well, you're in for a surprise. "Outer Banks Brewing Station" brings a different kind of excitement and positive energy to the table. With the talents of these highly acclaimed chefs, master brewer and owners, a unique brand of cuisine is now offered on the beach. They were the find wind powered brewery in the United States and the first business on the Outer Banks to produce wind power.

This brewery restaurant knows how to satisfy its customers. Everything they do is first class. For example, their brew master takes special care in selecting only the finest natural malt, hops and grains to brew their handcrafted beers. With the 17-barrel brewing system, this brew-master can brew up to 560 gallons of beer and soda at a time. You won't find better tasting beer anywhere, and if you just can't bring yourself to have a beer then try one of their own brewed sodas.

A combination of globally inspired dishes, the menu appeals to all tastes. Featured are rotisserie chicken, Atlantic seafood, steaks, Italian dishes and daily chef specials. Plus, their in-house pastry chef makes all of their desserts, breads, and cakes. So expect the best of the best, and that's what you'll get.

Aubrey's dream of owning a restaurant has finally become a reality. He's been collecting bricks for years from old cottages that have washed up on shore and even bricks from the old Third St. Grill restaurant that once was a part of the Sea Ranch Motel. Even the old historic Carolinian Hotel bricks now line the sidewalk of this restaurant and the old silo by the highway was salvaged from a Camden County farm. The restaurant is designed to represent a modern Life Saving Station, even the bricks on the floor are laid to look as if the 55 foot boat shaped bar is ready to be launched down the isle of bricks.

Live entertainment is featured year-round including jazz, folk music, and blues, blue grass, and acoustic. Children's menu available. Open daily year round for dinner and late night. Lunch served from memorial day thru labor day. Taste of the Beach 2011 winner of Peoples Choice-Overall, 2nd place for best dessert and 1st place for best booth presentation. This restaurant has won numerous awards over the years.

Pan Seared Hatteras Tuna

Served over Isralli Cous-Cous infused Caponata w/cornmeal fried oysters and Santa Claus melon relish

4   6 oz. portions of fresh Tuna
1   T. Olive oil
½   T. butter

Season Tuna with salt & pepper, heat large sauté pans over medium high heat with olive oil and butter till hot but not smoking. Add Tuna; sear 2-3 minutes on each side for rare, medium rare or until desired doneness.

Isralli Cous-Cous

½   red onion, small diced   1 ½ C. cous-cous
1   garlic clove, small diced   1 T. Olive oil
3   C. stock or water

Sauté onion and garlic in olive oil on medium heat until tender and caramelized, add cous-cous and slowly add stock 1/3 at a time, stirring frequently until cous-cous is aldente. Approximately 20 minutes. Pour on a sheet pan and cool.

Caponata

1 C. peeled-sliced-eggplant cut into ¼ thick-2 inch long pieces salted with 1 T. salt, let sit for 1 hour then pat dry. Salt and pepper to taste.

½ C. red onion, small, diced   1C. oven roasted tomatoes, small diced
½ C. red pepper, small diced   1 tsp. chili flakes
½ C. yellow pepper, small diced   3 T. pine nuts, toasted
1 C. zucchini, small diced   1 T. basil
1/3 C. olive oil   1 T. oregano
8 cloves garlic crushed   2 T. parsley
½ C. fennel bulb, small diced   lemon juice, to taste

*Sauté onions, bell peppers and zucchini in ½ the olive oil, remove the vegetables with a slotted spoon, drain in a colander.
*Heat the rest of the olive oil and the garlic, fennel and eggplant, cook several minutes until fork tender. Add oven-dried tomatoes. Mix in the chopped chili peppers and pine nuts, add the onion, pepper mixture and squeeze fresh lemon juice, season with salt and pepper—Stir

Santa Claus Melon Relish

½ red onion, small diced   1 ½ T. rice wine vinegar
1 clove garlic, crushed   1 T. sugar
2 small melons peeled, seeds removed, diced ¼ C. chopped chives

Toss all ingredients in mixing bowl-let stand for 15 minutes before using.
To present this dish; place cous-cous in the middle of the plate caponata on top, seared tuna on top of that and fried oysters around the plate and the melon relish on the very top of the tuna. *Enjoy*

The Brine & Bottle

7531 S. Virginia Dare Trail,   Nags Head-Manteo Causeway
Nags Head, North Carolina

Andrew Donovan, Executive Chef/Co-Owner   (252) 715-1818
Ashley Whitfield, Beverage Director/Co-Owner   www.thebrineandbottle.com

You'll find this great waterfront restaurant on the Manteo-Causeway in the brightly painted coral building. The Brine & Bottle specializes in seasonal Southern Cuisine at its finest by show casing fresh local ingredients from fisherman and farmers of Dare and nearby Currituck county in a small plate format. Dinner menu changes nightly.

Chef Andrew Donovan has already made a name for himself winning the Chef's Choice Award for the Taste of The Beach 2011. While working at the Sapphire Grill in Atlanta Georgia in 2005, he accepted an invitation to cook at the famed James Beard House's Savannah Nights dinner and in 2006 while cooking at the famous Core Club in Manhattan, Chef Donovan received a second invitation to cook at the James Beard House.

A collection of old bottles line the shelves in the dining area with a backdrop of a cobalt blue tiled bar that definitely will catch your eye. Dining on the waterfront deck overlooking the Roanoke Sound is a must while enjoying great food, fine wines.

The menu features soups, sandwiches, salads, seafood, duck, steaks, country ham, fried house pickles, Falls Mill grit cakes and so much more. For lunch try the fried Chesapeake oysters with roasted & pickled pepper salad or one of my favorites, shrimp & grits with Falls Mill grit cakes/ cava cream or the farmers plate of Benton's country ham with Thomasville tomme, assorted pickles, deviled eggs and saltines. Choose from small plate selections of shellfish bisque with diver scallops and poached NC oysters with shrimp broth or pan-seared flat iron steak or just a few of the many selections to select from.

The Brine and Bottle offers a list of fine wines. Just ask Ashley Whitfield, beverage director, which wines will pair well with your dinner selection. Micro and macro brew beers, etc… are also available. Open Monday thru Saturday for lunch and dinner in season. Call for winter hours. Catering services available onsite and offsite. Be sure and pick up one of their home canned vegetable jars for friends back home.

Apple-Cider & Citrus-braised Pork Shanks

(Serves 8)

8 bone-in pork shanks (14- 16oz each)
4 tablespoons canola oil
2 yellow onions, roughly chopped
4 carrots, peeled and chopped
6 cloves of garlic, smashed
juice of 2 each lemons & oranges
2 cups Sauvignon Blanc or other dry white wine
1 gallon fresh apple cider
2 cups water
kosher salt, to taste
fresh-ground black pepper, to taste

For Sachet
cheese cloth
twine
12 peppercorns
2 bay leaves
1 bunch thyme

Preheat oven to 275. Generously season pork shanks w/ kosher salt and fresh ground black pepper and set aside. Place a large oven-proof skillet on the stove over medium-high heat. Once hot, add canola oil and coat the pan.

In two batches, sear pork shanks on all sides until golden brown, adjusting heat as necessary to keep meat from scorching. Once shanks are seared on all sides, transfer them to a stainless steel hotel pan or other large oven-proof container. Drain hot oil from skillet and wipe surface clean with a kitchen towel. Return skillet to stovetop and set flame or burner temperature to medium. Add onions and cook until translucent, then add carrots and garlic and continue to cook for 3 to 4 minutes. Add in white wine and bring to a boil, then add apple cider, water, and juice from lemons and oranges. Add the sachet of herbs and spices and return liquid to a boil, then reduce heat and simmer for five minutes. Pour hot liquid over pork shanks in hotel pan, making sure that shanks are immersed. Cover with lid or aluminum foil and place into 275 degree oven. Cook until meat is almost falling off the bone but is still intact (about 4 hours). Remove shanks from pan and set aside, then strain the liquid into a deep sauce pot. Bring liquid to a simmer and cook until quantity is reduced by ½. Cool sauce quickly by immersing pot in an ice bath. Once the sauce has cooled, skim the fat from the surface.

To serve: Preheat oven to 400. Return liquid to a large oven-proof skillet and bring to a boil. Add in shanks and place into 400 degree oven. To keep meat from drying out while it warms, baste the shanks every five or six minutes by spooning hot liquid over the meat. When shanks are heated through (approximately 30 minutes), place skillet back on stovetop and turn heat to medium-high. Begin continuously basting the top of the shanks while sauce proceeds to thicken. When the sauce reaches the consistency where it coats and clings to the back of a spoon, the pork shanks are ready to serve.

I like to pair them with creamy stone ground grits and a nice seasonal vegetable, particularly caramelized Brussels sprouts during the cooler seasons.

Café Atlantic

P. O. Box 123, N.C. Hwy. 12
Ocracoke, North Carolina 27960
Bob and Ruth Toth, Owners   *(252) 928-4861*

This upscale and casual restaurant is located in a traditional beach-style building, but don't let that fool you. There is nothing traditional about the innovative way this restaurant prepares and serves their delicious, mouth-watering fares.

The views out across the marsh grasses and dunes are fantastic. The gallery-like effect is produced by the hand-colored photographs of local artist and writer, Ann Ehringhaus along with a great collection of artwork by Debbie Wells's on the second floor.

The lunch menu includes salads, sandwiches while the dinner menu offers combinations of fresh seafood, a wide range of beef, chicken, pasta plates. Sunday brunches are from 11 a.m. to 2 p.m.. Champagne and mimosas are always served. Make sure to save room for their outstanding desserts; this is to top off a delicious meal. Café Atlantic is open six days a week and closed on Tuesday's. Open from March thru October.

Sweet Potato Biscuits

2 medium-sized sweet potatoes	1 T. baking powder
(about 1 ¼ lbs.)	¼ tsp. salt
½ c. unsalted butter, melted (1 stick)	½ tsp. baking soda
¼ c. golden brown sugar (packed)	¼ tsp. ground cinnamon
2 ¼ c. all–purpose flour	2/3 c. buttermilk

Preheat oven to 400 degrees. Pierce potatoes in several places using a fork. Bake potatoes for about 1 hour until very tender. Cut potatoes in half and scoop out the pulp from the skins. Put potato pulp in a small bowl and cool completely. Reduce the oven temperature to 375 degrees. Place 1 cup sweet potato in a bowl, add brown sugar and butter, and beat until smooth. Sift flour, baking powder, salt, and cinnamon into medium bowl. Mix dry ingredients into sweet potato mixture alternately with buttermilk, in 3 additions, beginning and ending with dry ingredients. Transfer dough to generously floured surface. Roll to ¼ inch thickness. Using a 2 ¼ inch round cookie cutter, cut out biscuits. Arrange on baking sheet. Gather scraps into ball, re-roll to ¼ inch thick and cut out additional biscuits. Arrange on baking sheet. Bake biscuits until golden about 25 minutes. Makes about 12.

Café Franco's

1712 N. Croatan Highway, MP 7.5
Kill Devil Hills, North Carolina

www.CafeFrancos.com
(252) 255-2232

Franco & Beverly Mineo, Owners
Franco Mineo, Chef

The tradition of wonderful Italian cuisine continues with this restaurant inspired by the laid back lifestyle of the Italian people and good food. The atmosphere is both casual and inviting and it's the perfect place to enjoy a meal with family and friends.

Franco actually grew up in Silicy and knows a thing or two about real Italian food. You'll find him in the kitchen cooking up some of the best homemade Italian dishes you've ever tasted. The restaurant's menu captures the essence of rustic Italian recipes by using the finest local and imported ingredients to bring to you the best of Italy.

The menu features marvelous dining selections including great-tasting appetizers such as brushetta, pastas served with homemade bread and a great selection of entrees. For a special entrée, try the fettuccine portofino~ pan seared scallops, shrimp, clams tossed in a tomato-cream sauce served over fettuccine. Another great choice is gnocchi,~potato pasta tossed in a truffle shallot cream sauce.

Let's not forget about the wonderful "Panini" such as the meat ball parmmy or the godfather sub. Café Franco's has the best gourmet pizzas in the area with dough made fresh daily with filtered water. Create your own masterpiece here with a large choice of toppings. Franco's signature figgy pizza made with dried figs and gorgonzola cheese is definitely a favorite.

A full menu is available for the little bambini's. Wine and craft beers available. Open for lunch and dinner. Call for winter hours.

Fresh Bruschetta

6 roma tomatoes
3 cloves minced garlic
1/4 c. olive oil
2 tbsp. good balsamic vinegar

1/4 c. fresh, torn basil
1/4 tsp. salt
1/4 tsp. pepper

Sliced day old baguette or ciabatta bread.
Mix all ingredients in large bowl and allow to sit for 5 to 10 minutes. Divide mixture over bread slices.

Café Pamlico

"The Inn on Pamlico Sound"

49684 N.C. 12, Hwy, Buxton, N.C.

866-995-7030

www.innonpamlicosound.com

Steve Nelson, Owner   Restaurant— 252-995-4500

Forrest Paddock, Executive Chef   Suzette Caldiera, General Manager

Amidst all the beauty of the Pamlico Sound and the tranquil waterfront setting of "The Inn on Pamlico Sound" lies a world class casual elegant Inn and fine dining restaurant. The village of Buxton on Hatteras Island plays host to this European style hotel with the charm of a coastal bed and breakfast. Owner, Steve Nelson has created a retreat that is the perfect venue for a wedding, honeymoon, vacation, or group retreat.

Café Pamlico has become a destination for those wanting to experience gourmet fine dining while on the Outer Banks. Under the direction of Executive Chef Forrest Paddock, this restaurant has achieved notable recognition. Chef Paddock graduated from the prestigious Art Institute of Houston and later served a tour of nationally recognized kitchens before coming to the Cape Hatteras area in 2003.

The dining areas are split with the main dining area offering a feeling of intimacy in a classic retro setting or choose to dine on their large deck overlooking the sound. The décor of Café Pamlico is just as pleasing as the food. Chef Paddock prepares elegant gourmet dinners as well as elegant breakfasts fit for a king. Its location on Hatteras gives the chef access to local seafood unrivaled in freshness. A great supporting cast of poultry, organic beef, pastas, soups and salads, appetizers are also recommended. The portions are generous, and the presentation is impressive.

A great beginning to a memorable meal definitely is the Pamlico Sound Seafood Bisque followed by one of their signature dishes. The menu changes nightly, entrée selections may include "shrimp & grits" prepared with sautéed shrimp, andouille sausage, roasted tomatoes, mushrooms, and garlic over creamy cheese grits. Another great favorite is their pan seared lump crab cakes served with buttermilk mashed potatoes, grilled asparagus, and lemon horseradish aioli. Be sure and try the pan fried soft shell crabs when available in season. Vegetarian and young adult selections are available at each meal. The desserts are outstanding and are worth saving room for. In peak season the restaurant is open for an elegant breakfast, lunch and dinner and Sunday morning brunch.

If having a picnic at the beach, kayak ride, fishing charter are in your plans then let Café Pamlico prepare a simple or elegant picnic for your outing. A fine selection of wines is available to compliment your dining experience. The restaurant is open year round. Call for winter hours. Reservations are recommended in season as seating is limited but walk-ins are welcome.

The Inn is a great place to have a wedding overlooking the sound. Gourmet catering available for all special events.

Pan Roasted Muscovy Duck Breast
W/ Blackberry Balsamic Pan Jus

2   each duck breast
1   teaspoon fresh rosemary
1   teaspoon fresh thyme
1   teaspoon Sea salt
1   teaspoon fresh cracked black pepper
1   tablespoon minced shallots
6   oz. rich duck stock or light veal stock
2   oz. balsamic reduction
12 each fresh blackberries
1   tablespoon fresh butter

Place cast iron pan over medium heat. Score a cross hatch pattern in fat on duck breast; be sure not to cut through into the meat. Season duck breasts with half of fresh herbs, sea salt, and fresh cracked black pepper. Place the breasts, skin side down, into the dry cast iron pan.

Let the fat render from the breasts until its brown and crisp. Be patient it will take longer than you think—10 to 12 minutes. Flip the breasts and brown the other side. Cook to medium rare or medium.

Take the breast out of the pan and cover with foil. While the meat is resting, finish the pan sauce. Pour all but 1 tablespoon of the rendered duck fat, save the fat, it's great for sautéing. Add minced shallots and sweat till translucent, add remaining fresh herbs and blackberries. When the berries begin to pop and release their juices, deglaze the pan with stock. Add the balsamic reduction and reduce pan sauce by half. When sauce has reduced, finish with a pat of fresh butter. Slice duck breast, fan them on a warm plate, and spoon pan jus over and around the meat.

Capt'n Franks

U.S. Hwy 158, N. Croatan Hwy. M.P 4 ½
Kitty Hawk, North Carolina

Harvey and Kathleen Hess, Owners   (252) 261-9923
Harvey Hess, III, Head Chef and General Manager

Like to get a feeling for the way the Outer Banks used to be, to experience that atmosphere and sense of place? You need to go to Capt'n Franks. If any place at the beach can be called a landmark and an institution, Capt'n Franks is one of them.

When the Hess family built their restaurant in the sand dunes of Kitty Hawk, in 1974, Kitty Hawk was still just a place, not even a town. In 1975, Capt'n Franks opened its doors for its first summer, and now, 35 seasons later it has become an Outer Banks icon. In the beginning, Capt'n Franks was one of the first things you came to when you crossed the Wright Memorial Bridge, on a sand blown two-lane road, with dunes on both sides, and you can still look for the "Dancing Hotdog" on the sign at the 4.5 mile post in its original location.

Through all the change and growth, it has retained its sense of place, and sense of self. It is still located in the original building, with a few enhancements, and the Hess family, now in its third generation (Harvey, Sr., Harvey, Jr., and Harvey III) is still serving up what some people say is the best hotdog in the world. When asked about this, Harvey (aka Capt'n Frank) will tell you, "That's for other folks to judge, but somebody has to be the best, and maybe we are. Everybody ought to be great at something, we're great at hotdogs!"

Upon entering the building, you'll notice the sound, the noise and the smells of a bustling restaurant, and the vibes from the smiling staff, customers and the "grill". The walls are adorned with an eclectic collection of pictures of smiling and interesting people who have eaten here, from the very famous (Johnny Cash, John McEnroe, athletes, politicians) to all us normal folks who just like a great hotdog. Check out all those pictures of customers who have worn their Capt'n Franks T-Shirts all over the world.

Long known by locals as "the place" for a great hotdog , just ask one, Capt'n Franks is also known for its legendary, mouthwatering Eastern North Carolina 'hand pulled' Pit BBQ, and a menu of great sandwiches for any taste. Every menu item has been personally chosen for quality, flavor and presentation and must have "unanimous" approval by the Hess family before it crosses the counter to their customers.

You should also know, that "in season" Capt'n Franks is open until 9:00 PM Monday-Saturday (Sunday "Lunch Only") serving what many have said is simply the best "Steamed Shrimp" they have ever had. So every night from 4-9 pm, the shrimp is served steaming hot. And no shrimp is ever cooked until it's ordered, with the patron's choice of spices from mild to, let's say, very spicy! The regular menu is always available as well.

Capt'n Franks is extremely proud of its Outer Banks heritage and traditions, and is dedicated to keeping its philosophy of smiles, great food and great service alive and well. Family friendly, beach casual, and kids of all ages are always welcome.

Capt'n Franks is an experience you will think about when the Dogs of Winter are "chillin" your bones; don't miss it!

Chile Cheese Hotdog Pie

Ingredients:
2 cups of your favorite biscuit mix (Bisquick)
2/3 cup of water or milk
3 cups of chili with beans. (You want the chili kind of thick, so drain any excess liquid) "use canned products, but it is really easy to make your own."
1 pound of your favorite hotdogs, sliced into medallions about ¼ inch
2 cups (or more) of your favorite shredded cheese or cheeses

Directions:
1. Preheat oven to 350 degrees
2. Mix your baking mix to form a smooth dough (set aside)
3. Spread half of your chili mix into a 1 ½ quart casserole dish. Layer the hotdog medallions over the chili. Cover the medallions with cheese, and layer the remaining chili mix over the cheese.
4. Roll out your dough on a lightly floured surface to make a thin dough topping. Lay the dough over your pie and make a couple of holes in the dough to vent the steam.
5. Optional, (but I like it) add an additional topping crushed cheddar crackers (like Cheese Nips or Goldfish) to top off the dough
6. Bake for approx. 20-25 minutes or until the dough is golden brown.
7. Let cool for 10 minutes. *Serve with a cold crisp salad or raw vegetables with blue cheese or ranch dressing. Serves 4-6*

Chilli Peppers Restaurant

3001 N. Croatan Hwy. MP 5 ½
Kill Devil Hills, North Carolina

Jim Douglas, Owner   www.chilli-peppers.com   (252) 441-8081
Tony Calvio, Kitchen Manager   Heather Crum, Manager

This is the spot you're been looking for, serving creative cross culture cuisine with a flair for taste from around the world. The menu changes frequently, with daily lunch and dinner specials offered. Chilli Peppers is a casual, fun place with entertainment going on here late at night. A full bar is separated from the dining area and offers a nice wine selection, margaritas, and a variety of beer.

Some of my favorite entrees are the Chilli Peppers lump crab cakes and the incredible mix of grilled lobster, beef, shrimp and vegetables all on a skewer served over a Mediterranean tabbouleh. Try the nachos grande, it's a meal in itself. You will definitely want to save room for their in-house made from scratch desserts. From May thru October enjoy Tapas night every Thursday from 5-10 p.m.

Chilli Peppers is a 4-time winner of the Outer Banks Association Chowder Cookoff. They received the prestigious Scovie Award for their Award-Winning Cantaloupe Habanero Hot Sauce and have won many other International awards. Weekend brunches feature a Sunday Bloody Mary Brunch. Be sure and take home a bottle of Chilli's award-winning hot sauces and don't forget those famous Chilli Peppers T-shirts. Lunch and dinner are served seven days a week year round.

Be sure and check out their website for special events and yearly chili cook-off. Call for entertainment schedule. Happy hour daily from 3-5 p.m..

Chimmi Churry Oysters

For Chimmi Churry:

¼ lb. fresh cilantro   3 c. olive oil
4 bunch green onions   2 T. salt
1 T. minced garlic   1 T. black pepper

Mix all ingredients together in blender or food processor. Sauté 1 dozen shucked oysters in 2 T. butter. Add desired amount of Chimmi Churry and bring to boil. Plate and sprinkle with shredded fresh Parmesan and garnish with toast points. Yields 4 cups.

Colington Café

1029 Colington Road
Kill Devil Hills, North Carolina 27948
Carlen and Kenneth Pearl, Owners   (252) 480-1123

www.colingtoncafe.com

This popular restaurant is located only a mile off the bypass. Once you arrive, you'll feel as if you are stepping back in time with this Victorian style Café set high on a hill with its tranquil and unique setting amongst beautiful hundred year old live oaks. Southern Living rated it as Best Restaurant for the Best Price on the Outer Banks.

The Pearl's started out in a small sandwich shop on Colington road and two years later, moved to the present location. They converted the Victorian style home into a restaurant. It's unique in both its setting and its menu. The Café has four different small dining rooms, each with a different touch.

The menu specializes in fresh local seafood with a gourmet touch. With Carlen's French heritage, the menu has a French emphasis. Their renowned chefs are the best in the area bringing with them a new dimension of infusion cooking, with emphasis on fresh ingredients. The owners agree that they live in the best place for fresh ingredients---both seafood and produce. The menu also includes a wide selection of many beef, pork, chicken and pasta dishes. All deserts are made on premises. This popular restaurant is a "must do" and a favorite with locals.

Seafood Napoleon
Shrimp and Scallops in a Light cream sauce

1 lb. large shrimp	5 to 6 T. heavy cream
1 lb. medium scallops	1/8 C. sherry (cream) you can substitute
3 T. butter	white wine, but flavor won't be as
1 ½ T. flour	rich
½ small diced onion	

Sauté onion in butter for one minute. Put scallops and shrimp in. Keep heat medium high. Cook about 2 minutes. Sprinkle flour in pan. Cook a few seconds—pour sherry in. Cook down for about one minute. Pour in cream. If sauce needs thickening, remove seafood with slotted spoon. Cook down 2-3 minutes. Put seafood back in. Serve with rice. Serves 4-5 **Note:** Try not to use cooking sherry. A Taylor Cream sherry does great.

Darrell's Restaurant
Highway 64
Manteo, North Carolina

Allan and Lorana Daniels, Owners   (252) 473-5366

This restaurant has been serving people since 1960 and has been a favorite family-style eatery for locals as well as tourist. You'll always feel welcome here with the down-home atmosphere. There's even a 932 lb. Blue Marlin mounted on the wall.

Menu items include fresh local seafood, steaks, ribs and chops, chicken, appetizers, sandwiches and salads topped with oysters, tuna, shrimp or chicken. Two of my favorite soups are the Dare County Style Clam Chowder and the She Crab Soup. The fried oysters are the best in town. For breakfast try their new sweet potato hotcakes or the homemade three egg omelettes. Don't forget to try the fresh desserts, especially the hot fudge cake. Be sure and check the daily luncheon and dinner specials. A children's menu is also available. Darrell's is open year round for breakfast, lunch and dinner but closed on Sundays. Beer and wine available.

She Crab Soup

2 qt. half & half
1 pt. milk
1 lb. backfin crab meat
1 lb. regular crabmeat
1 c. self rising flour
½ stick margarine
1 tsp. chicken base
1/8 tsp. white pepper
¼ tsp. mace
¼ cup white cooking wine
salt to taste
1 tsp. shrimp base

Heat half & half and milk in heavy saucepan under low heat. Make a paste by adding margarine and flour. Add mixture to heated milk. Add all seasonings. After heating thoroughly, add crab meat and wine.

Diamond Shoals Restaurant & Seafood Market

46843 Hwy. 12
Buxton, North Carolina

Keith Gray, Owner
Seafood Market (252) 995-5521   Restaurant (252) 995-5217

Diamond Shoals has been a local favorite of tourist and landlubbers alike for as long as I can remember. Known for their fresh affordable seafood and for serving the best breakfast on the island. Plus, this outstanding recommendation is located on the beautiful Cape Hatteras National Seashore within sight of the Cape Hatteras Lighthouse.

This family style restaurant will definitely catch the attention of parents and children alike with the 200 gallon saltwater aquarium stocked with tropical and Gulf Stream sea life. A variety of marine creatures including anemones, corals and a four foot eel stand ready to be gazed upon.

The seafood is always fresh and delicious. In fact, they are so committed to freshness they even have there own seafood market in the same building where you can choose from the large selection of special catches of the day or bring in your own catch and have them cook it. Their friendly staff is proud to offer a product well respected.

Breakfast at Diamond Shoals is a favorite-you can tell by the parking lot, it's always full. Some of the menu offerings to choose from are pancakes, eggs, sausage, French toast, biscuits and gravy, seafood omelettes and more. Lunch is also a winner with a selection of seafood and regular wraps, lunch baskets of seafood served with fries and coleslaw, salads, burgers, sandwiches and their award winning clam chowder. Featured on the dinner menu is a variety of excellent entrees and seasonal specialties such as Diamond Shoals platter with shrimp, crab cake, grouper, scallops, calamari strips and oysters. Specialties of the house are very poplar and include stuffed shrimp or grouper dinner, linguine with pesto cream and snow crab legs. You'll also find Filet Mignon on the menu. Sushi is another favorite served daily and rolled fresh by the owner.

A children's menu is available. Wine and Beer served. Open for breakfast, lunch and dinner in summer and week-ends only in winter. Call for winter hours. Large orders of seafood –to– go available.

Diamond Shoals Famous Clam Chowder
(Makes 2 ½ gallons)

You will need a large stock pot for this recipe

Start with 2 ½ ounces of butter
½ chopped garlic
3 cups bacon (chopped very fine)
3 Bay leaves
Cook on high for five minutes, stirring often

Add
1 ¼ bunch celery (chopped fine)
2 ½ large yellow onions
1/8 cup of basil
Cook on high for 15 minutes, stirring often

Turn heat down to medium and;
Add 4 cups flour
Stir until flour disappears

Add clams and juice 76 ounces + (add more if you want more clams)
Stir all together

Add
1 ½ quarts half and half cream
2 quarts heavy cream
Stir all together

Add
1 ½ tsp. white pepper
1 ½ tsp. thyme
6 oz. clam base
Stir all together, Bring to a boil

Add ¾ quart of whole milk then take off

4 large potatoes
We cook the potatoes separate. Cut potatoes into bite size cubes. You can steam or boil potatoes. *Cook potatoes until just done. Add to chowder*

Dirty Dick's Crab House

Hwy. 158 Bypass MP 101/2   Hwy. 12, Avon Pier   Cape Hatteras
Nags Head, N.C.   Avon, N.C   Hatteras Landing- Ferry Dock
(252) 480-3425   www.dirtydickscrabs.com

Jack Frestal, Owner, Ken Hersey, Owner, Beany McGregor, Owner, Chef
Derek Dinkler, Owner, General Manager, Linda Livesey , Assistant General
Manager, Brian Frymire, Executive Chef

This restaurants name is definitely an eye catcher, but not to be confused with Dirty Dick's in Myrtle Beach. This restaurant is all about seafood with a New Orleans accent and one that you can take the whole family to. Well, even the t-shirts get your attention with the goofy looking fellow with the restaurant's motto "I got my crabs from Dirty Dick's" spread across the back of the shirt.

Dirty Dick's started out as a mere seafood take-out on the beach road in Kill Devil Hills and quickly became a favorite with tourist for their t-shirts and seafood to-go and later expanded to three restaurants on the Outer Banks. The atmosphere inside the new Nags Head location is both fun and casual with a more urban high tech look with a lot of stainless steel and bar seating for twenty one. The new location is definitely not a sports bar but geared to families. The Hatteras Ferry location is definitely a great place to have lunch or dinner while enjoying the endless views of the picturesque harbor and nature, no matter where you happen to be seated. You can catch a glimpse of the ferry as it leaves the dock or just watch the pristine charter boats bob in the gentle waves. The Avon location is another fun spot to gather with friends.

A large menu featuring everything from soups and salads, sandwiches, steamer items consisting of clams, snow crab legs, shrimp, Dungeness crabs and so much more is offered. From the Crab Pot, try fried crab lasagna or crab cakes, stuffed shrimp and crab. There are even regular entrees of BBQ. Fried green tomato parmesan, kabobs, ribs, chicken. Look for the specials of the day posted on the wall and the $5.99 lunch special.

Dirty Dick's is open seven days a week in season. Call for winter hours. Each location has a separate bar area with full ABC license. Clappy's Tiny Friends menu available for kids. Casual attire. Open for lunch and dinner.

Fried Potato Salad

This is one of the most popular items on the menu.

2.5 pounds baked potatoes, 1/2 inch cubes
3/4 cup mixed cheese, shredded
1/2 cup cooked bacon, chopped
1/2 cup green onions, sliced
1/2 cup warm bacon grease
1/2 cup ranch dressing
1/4 pound sour cream
1/8 cup black pepper

Add all ingredients except the cheese together and mix well by hand. Add the cheese when the potatoes are cool.
Portion in 6 oz. patties 1/2 inch high.

Make a bowl of egg wash, flour dish, and bread crumb dish.
Roll flour on pattie, put egg wash on pattie and finally cover with bread crumbs.

You can either sauté or deep fry in peanut oil until golden brown.

For presentation after finishing cooked pattie, top with cheese sour cream, crumbled bacon and green onion for garnish

In the recipe if you like more bacon, cheese, onion, etc, go ahead and add more to your taste.

Duck Deli

1378 Duck Road (N.C. Hwy. 12)
Duck, North Carolina

Ken Forlano, Owner   (252) 261-3354 or (252) 255-0861

In 2008, Duck Deli celebrates their 20th anniversary in business as a barbecue restaurant specializing in pork, beef, and chicken barbecue, which are still their specialties. Today, all the meats and fish are cooked daily using a hickory wood burning smoker. The sauces and marinades are a combination of local recipes with a little Duck Deli flair. Philly cheese steak subs, sandwiches, salads, hot dog and hamburgers are just a few of the choices you will find on their menu. A dessert menu of cobblers, brownies, shakes, and a frozen yogurt bar with plenty of toppings are available. A full breakfast menu includes everything from eggs, hot cakes, omelettes to cereal and bagels.

The Crab cake sandwich and the Smoked Mackerel cake sandwich are definitely worth trying. If you're real hungry, then try the B.B.Q Sampler platter that offers a combination of wings, ribs and pulled pork, or go for the full rack of pork ribs served with a choice of two vegetables and hushpuppies.

This popular casual Deli has become a favorite among the locals and tourist alike. You would feel comfortable dining in your bathing suit or shorts here. There's also an outside patio deck for dining. Prices are very reasonable. Take-out orders are prepared fresh for your enjoyment. Open for breakfast, lunch, dinner, in season. Fall and winter schedule may vary.

Smoked Tuna Salad

2 lbs. smoked tuna
½ c. sweet pickle relish
½ fresh lemon (juice with pulp)
1 c. celery, finely chopped
¼ c. onion, minced
Mayonnaise, added to the consistency you prefer.

Combine ingredients and serve as a tuna salad sandwich or on a bed of lettuce. Serves 6 to 8

The Dunes Restaurant

7013 S. Croatan Hwy. MP-16 1/2
Nags Head, North Carolina

Rufus & Roxie Pritchard, Owners   (252) 441-1600

The Dunes Restaurant has been a Nags Head tradition since it first opened in 1983. In the years since, it has been a meeting place for locals; a gathering place for far-flung, vacationing families; and always a warm and friendly dining institution for breakfast, lunch or dinner. Rufus and Roxie and the entire Dunes staff make it their goal to give every visitor a great dining experience. In fact, "Southern Living" magazine applauded how good The Dunes is, noting it's a "must place to stop on the Outer Banks…"

There are a lot of people who obviously agree because they come back year after year, eager to make the Dunes part of their Outer Banks vacation. Friendly faces, generous portions, fresh food cooked to order, and a warm family atmosphere are trademarks of The Dunes Restaurant. Their menu features salads, soups, sandwiches, seafood, steaks, poultry, and pastas.

The restaurant has taken on a new facade with the recent remodeling in 2010 giving the restaurant additional seating and a great new look. A new, state-of-the-art, "R" Bar and cocktail lounge were added making it perfect for grabbing a mixed drink, glass of wine or beer while waiting for a table. Lighter fare is also available in the "R" Bar as well as the full Dunes' menu.

The Dunes specialize in big breakfasts. There's also a popular breakfast and fresh fruit bar that's a favorite and available daily April thru October (weekends year round). A child's menu is also available. On premise catering for up to 250 people.

Beulah's Squash Casserole

1 ½ lbs. fresh squash	2 T. butter or margarine, melted
¼ tsp. pepper	1 c. Parmesan cheese
½ c. chopped onion	¾ c. French bread crumbs
1/8 tsp. salt	2 eggs
1 c. mayonnaise	

Sauté squash and onion until tender. Drain well. Combine squash and onion with mayonnaise, cheese, eggs, and seasonings. Mix well and pour into casserole dish. Mix butter and bread crumbs until crumbly (add more crumbs if necessary). Sprinkle bread crumbs on top of squash. Bake 30 minutes at 350 degrees. This is the best. Serves 4-6.

Elizabeth's Café & Winery

Scarborough Faire Shoppes
Duck, North Carolina

Leonard G. Logan, Jr., Proprietor   (252) 261-6145
Brad Price, Executive Chef   Shawn Pennington, Sous Chef

This quaint bistro nestled among the pines of Scarborough Faire has received accolades from their reviewers and guests as "one of the finest restaurants in the world for the pairing of food and wine." Elizabeth's has earned international acclaim as one of only 329 restaurants in the world to receive the Best of Award of Excellence by The Wine Spectator. The Wine Enthusiast awarded this restaurant "The Award of Ultimate Distinction" for years 2004 and 2005.

Elizabeth's is a cozy, warm and delightful place to dine. There's even a fireplace that's usually lit on cool evenings. Only a handful of restaurants in the world offer an a la carte menu and two prix fixe wine dinners (six course meals with accompanying wines) nightly. The restaurant has a walk-in wine cellar and offers a tasting wine bar in season where you can try a wine before buying a bottle or case to go. Wine tasting is by appointment in off season. Winemakers from around the world are sometimes featured here for special dinners. Elizabeth's offers an extensive selection of wines in their wine shop.

Chef Price takes his cooking cues from wine pairings. His knowledge of countless wines, his ability to pair the perfect wine with each dish makes every dish a magical one. He has been named for the past four years by the International Restaurant & Hospitality rating bureau as one of America's top 100 chefs.

Southern Living magazine said "Elizabeth's Café and Winery is Country French and Sensational. It's also some of the best food you're likely to find on the Outer Banks." The menu changes nightly and reflects the chef's daily purchases. Only at this restaurant will you enjoy some of the freshest ingredients of the day. A pastry chef creates different desserts daily.

Elizabeth's is open for dinner six nights a week in season and closed on Sunday. Call for winter hours in off season. This café is so popular that you will want to make your reservations early. <u>Reservations in season are a must.</u>

Vidalia Onion Tart
(Serves 12-16)

Filling:
5 Vidalia onions, sliced (large)
1 qt. heavy cream
2 shallots, chopped
1 lb. goat cheese, crumbled
salt & pepper to taste
6 eggs

Cook sliced Vidalia onions and shallots on high heat, sauté until caramelized, then reduce heat to low and add heavy cream, simmer for 15 to 20 minutes. Add goat cheese to mixture, then turn heat off and let blend together. Beat the 6 eggs in a bowl and slowly add to mixture already made.

Crust:
Tart shell recommended or deep dish pie pan can be used
2 cups pecans, finely chopped
2 cups graham cracker crumbs
1 egg white, blended into mixture of nuts and crumbs
Take mixture and press into bottom of tart shells or pie pan that has been sprayed with Pam or similar product. Bake at 375 degrees for 10 minutes.
Once shell has cooked, take out of oven and cool 5 minutes, and then add filling mixture.
Cook in oven at 350 degrees for about 30 to 40 minutes, (should turn nice golden color, mixture should be firm.)

Sauce:
Balsamic vinegar--- 4 oz. put in pan on medium heat, reduce to a syrup consistency. Then drizzle over tarts when ready to serve.

1587 Restaurant

At the Tranquil House Inn
Queen Elizabeth Avenue
Manteo, North Carolina

Donnie Just, General Manager   (252) 473-1587
Donny King, Chef, Manager Consultant
James Lee, Chef de cuisine   Brent Bartlett, Sous Chef

www.1587.com

1587 Restaurant is located in the Tranquil House Inn on the Manteo waterfront. Just minutes from the special attractions, old and new, found in Manteo, they provide an atmosphere that is both comfortable and intriguing. Upon entering the restaurant, you will find exciting food and interesting wines paired with a professional and upbeat level of service. Their chefs offer creative twists to familiar foods including fresh local ingredients. Southern Living describes it a "remarkably creative cuisine." Their wine list has also been recognized in Wine Spectator with their annual "Award of Excellence." In an area where locals know and value great restaurants, their friendly staff is proud to offer a product well respected. This recipe is one of many unique dishes you can learn about when you sit near their open kitchen and view the skilled and dramatic creation of their cuisine.

They are as equally proud of their restaurant, and the service it provides, as they are the Tranquil House Inn. You will find a beautiful twenty-five room bed and breakfast with individually decorated rooms and many fine amenities. After dinner, stroll along the marina and admire the charming and comfortable surroundings, or finish the night with an evening libation on their large open deck overlooking Shallowbag Bay. Open year round. Reservations are highly recommended in season.

Cornmeal Crusted Softshell Crabs with Wild Rice, Vidalia Onion-Tomato Cream, and Cucumber-Feta Salad

Vidalia Onion-Tomato Cream

2 Tbsp. Olive Oil (extra Virgin if available)
½ large Vidalia onion, large dice
2 cloves garlic, minced
2 ripe large tomatoes, large dice

½ cup heavy cream
8 leaves fresh basil, shredded
salt and pepper

In a small saucepan, heat the olive oil and sauté the Vidalia onion on medium to high heat until it is translucent. Add the garlic and stir for a minute or two. Add the tomatoes and let simmer for about ten minutes, stirring occasionally. Puree the tomatoes and onions in a blender and place back in the saucepan on the stove. Stir in heavy cream and fresh basil and keep on medium heat until almost to a boil. Taste, season with salt and pepper and set aside.

Cucumber-Feta Salad

½ large Vidalia onion, julienne
1 cucumber, halved, seeded and sliced
2 ripe Roma tomatoes, seeded and sliced
2 Tbsp. red wine vinegar

4 Tbsp. olive oil
1 Tbsp. salt and pepper
2 oz. Feta cheese

Julienne the Vidalia onion (cut into very thin strips) and place in a stainless mixing bowl with the vinegar, oil, salt, and pepper. Cut the cucumbers and tomato strips and toss with the onions and vinaigrette. Finally crumble in the Feta cheese and give one final toss.

Softshell Crabs

8 jumbo softshell crabs, cleaned
3 eggs, whisked with ¾ cup water
2 cups flour
2 cups cornmeal
1 Tbsp. slat and pepper

Season the flour with the salt and pepper and dredge the cleaned softshell crabs in the flour. Then place them in the eggwash (whisked water and egg mixture). Finally, dredge them through the cornmeal and set them aside on the plate.

To Plate: Prepare two cups rice to your specifications. Heat two large sauté pans with about ¼ cup vegetable oil in each on high heat until very hot. Place the coated softshell crabs into the pans, two at a time, and cook each side to a golden brown. Don't forget to season the crabs again. Place on a large oven tray when done and repeat the process. Make sure rice and sauce are hot and place the softshells in a 375 degree oven for about five minutes. Place a large spoon full of wild rice in the center of four large plates. Surround the rice with _Vidalia-Tomato Cream_. Remove the softshell crabs from the oven and place two on each mound of rice. Finally, top each entrée with an equal amount of _Cucumber-Feta Salad._

Fishbones Raw Bar & Restaurant

1171 Duck Road
Duck, North Carolina

John Kotch, Owner

(252) 261-6991

Zach Larrimore, Executive Chef

This Bahamian-inspired eatery is located upstairs in the Scarborough Lane Shopping complex in Duck. Fishbones was Duck's first original Outer Banks-style Raw Bar, serving raw and steamed seafood. An always popular spot, this restaurant is always busy in season as the bar stretches the entire length of the dining area. It's a great place to meet friends and enjoy good food prepared by one of Outer Banks best chefs.

There's an extensive menu offering beef, chicken, pork and seafood prepared natural or with Caribbean sauces. Their Hatteras style Clam chowder won first place in the Outer Banks 1st Annual Chowder Cookoff!! Lunch entrees include sandwiches, soups, seafood baskets, burgers and specials of the day. For dinner, try the Seafood Alfredo made with a medley of tuna, shrimp and scallops tossed with linguine and homemade Alfredo sauce with parmesan cheese. Fishbones is open year-round for lunch and dinner. Be sure and visit their other Restaurant, "Fishbones Sunset Grill & Raw Bar" located on the Currituck Sound, Duck road in Duck. Fantastic views and great times await you at their new restaurant.

Fishbones Spicy Crab Dip

2 lbs. crab meat
2 lbs. cream cheese
2 cups heavy cream
½ cup culinary cream
9 oz. sherry
pinch of Old Bay
pinch of white pepper
1 T. Schreiher crab base
1 tsp. flaming ass (or hot sauce)

Place cream cheese in mixer with paddle and beat about 2 minutes. Scrape bowl while running mixer. Add heavy cream and sherry. Turn off and scrape bowl. Turn on low and add picked crab meat, Old Bay and white pepper. Scrape into container. Refrigerate.

Fishbones Sunset Grille & Raw Bar

1264 Duck Road
Duck, North Carolina

John Kotch, Owner

Sean Mccaffry, Executive Chef

Thomas Seehafer, Sous Chef

(252) 261-3901

General Manager, Paige Gaddy

Located in the heart of the now famous Duck Village, this sound side restaurant overlooks the beautiful Currituck Sound. Here you can enjoy fabulous sunsets and delightful views through the wall of glass windows while enjoying excellent regional cuisine. An, if you didn't already guess, Sunset Grille gets its name from those breathtaking sunsets. This restaurant is a lively fun place to meet friends or just hang out with the gang. There's a huge deck with outdoor seating on the waterfront, a 40 foot gazebo that sits in the Sound and an outside tiki bar serving unique island- style cocktails. This is a Jimmy Buffet kind of place.

Sunset Grill is the sister restaurant to Fishbones Raw Bar & Grill, also located in Duck. Like Fishbones, the theme here is also Caribbean an entrees and appetizers reflect it. This award winning restaurant serves up the freshest seafood available along with pastas, choice steaks, barbecue ribs, chicken and a great selection of appetizers. Breakfast is available in season and week-ends in off season. Breakfast isn't the usual fare here. Skillet dishes, omelets, smoked salmon bagels, colossal biscuits topped with eggs and cheese are just a few of the breakfast items. The lunch menu has delicious sandwiches, soups and salads to choose from along with a selection of seafood and other favorites. For dinner, try the Cajun stuffed shrimp or the fresh fish of the day. There's just so much to choose from on their menu. The raw & steam bar serves all the favorites, oysters, clams, lobster etc...

Sunset Grille is known for its extensive drink menu. Specialty drinks are served Key West style in novelty glasses. No lack of bars at Sunset, there's a full bar upstairs shaped in the form of a horseshoe, a bar on the first floor and a tiki bar on the outside deck. An extensive wine list is available.

Meals are served down stairs or upstairs and even outside on the deck. A children's menu is provided. Whatever your mode of transportation—boat, bike, drive, walks—Sunset Grill is a place you'll cherish memories of for a lifetime. Call for winter hours. Open daily in season for breakfast, lunch and dinner. This is a busy restaurant. Call ahead for wait time.

Sunset Grille Coconut Curry Lobster
Four Servings

4   1 to 1 1/4 lb. cooked Maine Lobster
   or 4 6 to 8oz. cooked lobster tails

Remove claws from Maine lobster and reserve meat. Split lobster bodies in half—remove meat and reserve shells. On Maine lobster remove sack behind head and discard. Cut cooked lobster meat into 3/4 inch pieces and reserve.

Sauté in butter ½ cup diced onion, 2 tsp. chopped garlic
add a few sliced mushrooms, a little chopped tomato and the cooked lobster meat.

Add:
2 tsp. curry powder (more or less depending on your taste)
Lightly sauté and add a little white wine
1 cup chicken broth
4 tbsp. Coco Lopez (the stuff you use for Pina Coladas) salt and pepper to taste. Remove meat from sauce and arrange in the reserved shells.

Add 1 cup heavy whipping cream to sauce and cook, stirring constantly until thickened. Spoon sauce over lobster meat in shells and serve immediately or hold in a warm oven.

Serve with rice, Caribbean style black beans and fresh vegetables

Fish House Restaurant

Highway 12 (on the Harbor)
Buxton, North Carolina

Oden Family, Owners
Heidi Blackwood, Manager   (252) 995 5151

If you are looking for a black tie restaurant, Fish House Restaurant is probably not for you; but if you are looking for a restaurant that provides seafood dishes cooked in the traditional Outer Banks style, you won't be disappointed. Thirty -six years ago this restaurant was a "fish house." Look closely and you will notice that the floor slants toward the sound. This was done on purpose so the water from the fish boxes would drain back into the sound.

It's been a restaurant every since, and well known to Hatteras Island locals and visitors for its fresh seafood.   Some changes have occurred since it was known as "Billy's Fish House" but the restaurant still gets it seafood from the local commercial fishermen. They still use plastic dinnerware to avoid the damage that a dishwasher would cause to the aquatic life.

Visit this one of a kind restaurant and sit back and enjoy the views of the harbor and the Pamlico Sound in the distance. You will have a fun time, eat good food, and add a pleasant memory to your Outer Banks adventure.

Crab Cakes

1 lb. Backfin crabmeat	¼ tsp. salt
2 T. Hellman's mayonnaise	1 egg beaten
1 T. Dijon mustard	2 T. butter
1 tsp. Worcestershire	1 T. oil
1 T. parsley	Seafood breader

Mix mayonnaise, mustard, Worcestershire, parsley, salt and egg. Add crabmeat, mix gently. Make into crab cakes then gently bread. Heat butter, oil in skillet. Add cakes and cook 3 to 4 minutes on medium heat on each side.

Flying Fish Café

2003 S. Croatan Highway, 158 Bypass, MP 10
Kill Devil Hills, North Carolina

Owners, Bobby & Tiffany Starkey   Owners, Ryan & Shelley DeBerry
Rob Matis, Head Chef   *www.flyingfishfobx.com*
(252) 441-6894

The Flying Fish Café is a year round coastal restaurant that offers you a taste of American and Mediterranean inspired specialties. It is a dynamic value oriented restaurant that specializes in fresh local seafood, lean meat and poultry, plus unique vegetarian dishes. "From scratch" signature dishes comprise the majority of the menu. The pastry chef will temp you with desserts like the Chocolate Hurricane and the Grecian Urn. They also feature a wide choice of expresso and cappuccino drinks. It is easy to see why this restaurant has won a place in the hearts of those who have dined here. It is casual, yet elegant, hosting wonderful service and elegant presentation of the food with careful attention to detail.

Not to be overlooked is the extensive wine list with over 40 wines available by the glass or bottle. Flying Fish Café has been awarded The Wine Spectator Award of Excellence for its fine wine list and also was featured on the Food Network under the "Best of Cafes" segment for the year 2000. They also received "Best in Show" Taste of the Beach 2004. Open for dinner year round, seven nights a week. Reservations suggested in season.

Italian Cream Cake

(Serves 10)   Prep Time: 35minutes

1/2 cup shortening, room temp
1 stick butter, room temp
2 cups sugar
5 eggs, separated & room temp
2 cups flour
1 teaspoon baking soda
1/2 teaspoon salt
1 cup buttermilk, room temp
2 cups shredded coconut
1 cup finely chopped pecans or walnuts
1 teaspoon vanilla extract

Directions:

Preheat over 325 degrees and grease and flour (3) 9 inch cake pans
In the bowl of an electric mixer cream the shortening, butter and sugar
until light and fluffy
Add the egg yolks 1 at a time, beating well, sift the flour baking soda
and salt together onto a sheet of waxed paper
With the mixer on low speed, add the sifted ingredients in the batches
alternately with the buttermilk
In a separate bowl, beat the egg whites until stiff, and gently fold into
the prepared batter
Add the coconut pecans and vanilla into batter
Divide the batter among 3 pans and bake 25 minutes
Allow cakes to cool for 10 minutes then stack the layers with frosting
on top and sides
While cake baking, prepare frosting

Frosting

1 8oz package cream cheese
1/4 cup butter, softened room temp
1 teaspoon vanilla
1 16oz box powdered sugar, sifted
3/4 cup finely chopped pecans or walnuts

Combine cream cheese, butter and vanilla using electric mixer beat
until smooth and creamy
Add sifted powdered sugar and mix, add nuts and fold together

Full Moon Café & Brewery

208 Queen Elizabeth Avenue and Sir Walter Raleigh
Manteo, North Carolina

www.thefullmooncafe.com   (252) 473-6666

Sharon Enoch & Paul Charron, Chef-Owners

Nestled in the heart of downtown Manteo, under the town tower lies a legendary Café where the location is exceptional and the food is sublime. Amidst the quaint seaside town The Full Moon Café opened its doors in the fall of 1995 to the rave reviews of locals and tourists. In an area known for outstanding seafood, the cheflowners of the café brought their own special twist to the local cuisine adding international sauces and culinary favorites from around the world. Seafood, fresh and intriguing sauces, imaginative soups, huge salads, tempting sandwiches and the largest selection of vegetarian entrees in the area dot this interesting and well-balanced menu.

Sharon and Paul invite everyone to come to Manteo and enjoy a wonderful afternoon of shopping, strolling, bird watching, and visiting on e of North Carolina's premiere historic sites: Festival Park and the Elizabeth II. Take a break during the day to relax in their jewel of a dining room, enjoy great food, and savor every moment that the Outer Banks has to offer. The Full Moon Café is open year round, but the hours are seasonal so call ahead to reserve a table.

The following recipe for Mushroom Gorgonzola soup was developed by Sharon as many recipes were and still are: she looks around the kitchen, sees what is handy and concocts. It is said that baking is a science, but true cooking comes from the heart. It is in this spirit that this recipe is tendered…experiment and add, substitute and augment, stir, taste and add some more. Nothing is written in stone. However, Sharon has one rule; She always starts with an onion...

The Full Moon Café & Brewery specializes in British and Irish style beers. There's also a variety of North Carolina draft beers available. Tours of the brewery are by request.

Mushroom Gorgonzola Soup

1 medium onion
2 stalks celery
2 T. butter
1 T. chicken or vegetable base
1 tsp. dill (dried)
1 lb. mushrooms (white, portobella or shiitake: the greater the variety, the greater the complexity)

1 qt. heavy cream or milk
1 qt. water
2 T. flour or yellow cornmeal
Salt and pepper
4 oz. gorgonzola cheese

Sauté the onions and celery until translucent. Add sliced mushrooms and sauté until limp. Add the flour or cornmeal, base and dill, and sauté for 5 minutes. Add the water, then the milk or cream, and reduce heat. Do not boil at this point or the soup will curdle. Crumble the gorgonzola and add, leaving enough time before serving for the cheese to melt. At this point you could also add some drained frozen spinach, basil or corn. Again, the basics of soup making are sautéing veggies and adding stock, so create away and let your imagination run wild.

The Good Life Eatery

3712 N. Croatan Hwy. Unit A,   MP 4 ½
Kitty Hawk, North Carolina

Steve and Susie Mace, Owners
Stevie Mace III, Owner, Wine Expert

(252) 480-2855
www.goodlifegourmet.com

The Good Life name really describes this great eating establishment. The feeling created here is one of a very unique urban setting with a backdrop of a flat wall waterfall located over the fireplace in the dining area, large windows surround on three sides inviting diners to relax with friends in a casual serene setting. The outdoor covered patio courtyard is also a great place to have a glass of wine and grab a quick lunch.

The Good Life is a mixture of gourmet food items, coffee, wine and cheese shop, eatery, bakery, deli an espresso & cappuccino bar, gift baskets. It's the sort of place you might find in Atlanta or New York, but on the Outer Banks you'll find this great eatery in the former site of the Beach Bread Company. It's a very popular place for breakfast, lunch and evening dining, or just to enjoy breakfast muffins and pastries. Breakfast is big here with the all new "Frying Pan breakfast" served in a real frying pan. Now that's different! Try the Confederate Johnny cakes, crepes, sourdough pancakes or build your own omelet.

To give you a taste of the "Good Life" menu, if you hunger for a great sandwich, you'll want to order the grilled chicken salad & apples with raisins and curry mayonnaise on whole wheat. Another favorite is the smoked turkey & Applewood bacon with Tillamook cheddar, green apple and basil mayonnaise on French bread. Others recommended include the warm roast pork and country ham with jalapeno jack cheese, guacamole and black beans on a potato brioche roll. Classic deli sandwiches are made to order the way you like' em. New to the menu is the Philadelphia style grinder/hoagie. It's definitely a favorite, but there's also the smoked turkey, tuna, beef & blue, and the list goes on….The grilled Panini's served on pita bread w/chips and a pickle are great choices also. The menu also features a number of vegetarian favorites and low-carb dishes. All breads and pastries are baked fresh daily on premises.

If you love salads, order their grilled chicken salad with apples, raisins and curry mayonnaise or the blue cheese salad with crumbled blue cheese, egg, red peppers, carrot, onion, tomato, cucumber and blue cheese dressing. Try one of their great tasting soups of the day. There's so much to choose from on the menu to temp the palate at the "Good Life". Oh, and those great deserts!! In 2011, The Taste of the Beach People's Choice Award for Best Dessert third place winner was awarded to the Good Life. The chocolate flourless espresso cake is a favorite along with the homemade pies, cakes, cookies.

Stevie's wine shop contains more than 150 wine selections, at least a dozen of which are served by the glass. The large bar also offers a fine selection of distinctive beers and extensive line of microbrews. The Good Life Gourmet was voted the 2002 Chili Cook-off winner in the vegetarian chili category with their very popular "Fool Ya' vegetarian chili."

Everything they serve is available for take out. Call in orders are welcome. Definitely consider" Good Life Gourmet" catering service for your beach parties, weddings, and any other special event. They offer full service bartending, formal or informal as needed, custom catering making anything that is requested for small and large events. The Good Life is one of the premier caterers on the Outer Banks and has been for many years.

Kids menu available. Open year round serving breakfast, lunch and dinner. Call for off-season hours. Don't forget that **wi-fi** *access is available here. The Good Life Gourmet is definitely the "Best kept secret on the beach.*

Good Life Tuna Salad

2 ½ lbs. fresh tuna
1/8 cup lemon juice
2 ribs of celery (diced finely)
½ medium yellow onion
1/8 cup red wine vinegar
1 cup mayonnaise
½ cup Dijon mustard
½ cup toasted almonds
1 cup of split grapes
1 tablespoon diced fresh dill
1 tablespoon Old Bay seasoning
D*irections*: Boil tuna, drain, let cool, chop remaining ingredients and blend with tuna. (*This is the house recipe*)

Goombay's Grill & Raw Bar

1608 N. Virginia Dare Trail MP 7
Kill Devil Hills, North Carolina 27948

Karen & Charles Hennigan   (252) 441-6001

Know on the Outer Banks as a fun place for good food, drinks and just a great place to hang out. Locals love this place. The ambiance is upbeat and casual with bright and colorful surroundings. A wall size tropical mural covers one wall of the dining area. The horseshoe shaped bar is a great place to have a drink and try some of the great appetizers. A raw bar is open until late serving steamed shrimp, oysters, and many other favorites.

Goombay's serves great local seafood with a Caribbean eclectic influence. A variety of foods anywhere from Asian to Cajun to Continental can be found here. For lunch, try one of the specials of the day or a great hamburger, sandwiches, coconut shrimp or my favorite, jazzy coconut chicken. Call for entertainment schedule. Open for lunch and dinner year round. Kid friendly.

Goombay's West Indian Curried Chicken

8 boneless, skinless chicken breast halves	1 T. Curry powder
1 c. raisins	1 T. allspice
2 to 3 bananas, peeled and sliced	1 T. ground coriander
Sauce	1 T. Granulated garlic
1 qt. heavy cream	(garlic powder)
5 oz. cream of coconut (Coco Lopez	1 T. cayenne pepper
or other)	2 T. salt

Pound chicken breasts until ¼ in. thick. Make sauce by melting cream of coconut in a bowl and adding dry ingredients; mix thoroughly. Whip in cream until smooth. Heat 1 or 2 T. of clarified butter or oil in sauté pan over medium-high neat. When just smoking, add chicken breasts. (May need 2 batches, depending on pan size.) Sauté breasts for 2 or 3 minutes; turn and sauté for an additional 2 minutes. Add raisins and bananas. Add sauce and cook for an additional 2 or 3 minutes or until chicken is done. Plate chicken and reduce sauce for another minute or so until desired consistency is obtained. Pour sauce equally over breasts and garnish with a tablespoon of Major Grey's Chutney and flaked coconut. Serves 4 to 8.

The Great American Grill

(Located in the Hilton Garden Inn)
5323 Virginia Dare Trail, North
Kitty Hawk, North Carolina

Greg Sniegowski, Executive Chef   1-877-629-4586 or (252) 261-1290
April Schisser, Sous Chef   Karl Yearly, Sous Chef
Robin Rector, Food and Beverage Director

The Hilton Garden Inn has finally arrived at the oceanfront along with "The Great American Grill", a much needed restaurant and hotel on this end of the beach. The Taste of the Beach 2011 awarded this restaurant, "Best Outer Banks Cuisine and Best in Show." Pleasurably elegant and relaxing, the large dining area offers views of the ocean, courtyard and dolphins fountain in the distance. The Hilton also offers elegant banquet facilities for up to 325 guests, Guest will enjoy strolling out on the old "Kitty Hawk Pier", now a part of the Hilton facilities, just to gaze or sit and enjoy the ocean views. During hurricane Isabel, a large section of the pier was destroyed and today the section that remains is for the enjoyment of Hilton guest.

A great start for the day is their open breakfast buffet, where you can watch your food being prepared and have your omelette, just the way you like it. For lunch, the open face crab melt sandwich and the Mobley burger, named after Conrad Hilton's first hotel, are a must try along with the chicken monterey sandwich. All sandwiches and burgers come with choice of fries, fruit, or cottage cheese. Soups, salads, burgers, and appetizers are also served. The dinner menu features seafood, pasta, filet mignon, rib-eye steaks, chicken, and pizza. The jumbo stuffed shrimp stuffed with Carolina crab meat is definitely a favorite you'll want to try. Your server will be delighted to describe the chef's special selection of the day. Why not complement your dining experience with a glass of white or red wine.

Be sure and visit the Pavillion lounge. Full ABClicense. Open year round serving a breakfast buffet, lunch and dinner. Children's menu available.

Crab Cakes

4 cans lump crab meat	1 tsp granulated garlic
¾ cup diced roasted red pepper	1 tsp onion powder
1 cup mayonnaise	1 tsp salt
¾ cup liquid egg	2 T. lemon juice
2 T. dried parsley	2 cups Panko bread crumbs
1 T. dried mustard	

Mix the mayo, eggs, red pepper, and the rest of the seasonings together. Then add the bread crumbs to the mixture and mix. Then add the crab meat, make sure to mix gently to keep the crab lumps together as much as possible.

Grits Grill

Outer Banks Mall, North Wing
Nags Head, North Carolina

Rufus & Roxie Pritchard, Owners gritsgrill365@msn.com
Patrick Pritchard, Manager (252) 449-2888

If grits are on your mind and you're looking for a real southern tradition, then head on down to Grits Grill. This is where you'll find the locals and tourist having breakfast or lunch. Grits opens at 6:00 a.m. serving fresh Krispy Kreme donuts, omelettes, pancakes, grits and even lunch items. It's one of the few places on the beach that you can order anything on the menu from early morning till closing. Grab a seat at the bar and watch your breakfast being prepared in front of you. Definitely a busy place in season, you never know who you'll run into. On one of my visits, an old friend of my daughters from 30 years ago spotted me after all those years. Grits is definitely a great place to meet, eat and greet.

Breakfast is definitely a favorite here, with the famous "kiss our grits" served with 2 eggs, 2 pancakes, choice of hash browns or grits and bacon or sausage. Add a few cents more and try any of their cheddar, bacon, or sausage gourmet grits. Shrimp and grits are the star attraction here with creamy shrimp in white sauce served over grits, toast or biscuit. Steak and eggs and the country ham platter are also offered with grits. If you love seafood, then you'll want to try their seafood omelette made with shrimp, crabmeat and swiss, it's a favorite. Pancakes are huge and cover most of the plate, just add blueberries, pecans or chocolate chips for a different taste.

Appetizers, soups, salads, sandwiches and blue plate specials are on the lunch menu but are available any time. The popcorn shrimp is a hot lunch item along with the beach burger, Nags Head burger, homemade chicken salad and crabcake sandwich. The clam chowder is also homemade and a favorite.

Don't forget to say hello to Sandy Midgett, she's been there for years and always has a big smile on her face. Open year round for breakfast and lunch from 6:00 a.m. to 3:00p.m. Little grits menu available.

Roxie's Shrimp n' Grits

3 lbs. popcorn shrimp 1 large onion, finely diced
1 lemon squeezed 1 medium green pepper, finely diced
ground cayenne pepper, a (little salt) 5 strips crisp bacon
½ cup bacon grease

Place shrimp in a bowl, sprinkle with cayenne pepper and a little salt-set aside. In a skillet over medium heat, heat the bacon drippings, sauté the onion and green pepper until the onion begins to look translucent, about 10 minutes. Add the shrimp and sauté till pink (do not overcook). Crumble about 5 pieces of crisp bacon. Add the mixture to the sausage and gravy mix = YUMMY!!

Henry's Beef and Seafood
Hwy 158 Bypass MP 5
Kill Devil Hills, North Carolina MP

Henry and Linda Ezzell, Owners   **(252)261-2025**

Henry's is a great place for families to dine in a casual atmosphere. Open seven days a week year round serving Breakfast, Lunch and Dinner with specials offered daily. Senior citizens menus are also available. This is a favorite restaurant for locals to meet with friends for breakfast. Menu choices feature basic American fare specializing in broiled or fried seafood, chicken, pasta, and prime rib or steaks.

In business here for 15 years, the Ezzells offer good food at a reasonable price. A separate non-smoking room is available, all ABC permits. Restaurant is closed on Sunday's during off season.

Brownie Pie
(recipe makes four 9" pies)

1 ½ lbs. Butter or Oleo
12 oz unsweetened chocolate
12 eggs
6 cups sugar
4 TBS vanilla
3 cups sifted self-rising flour

Melt butter and chocolate, add eggs and stir til smooth
Add sugar, vanilla, and flour
Wisk till well blended and pour into 9" pans
Bake at 350 degrees for 22-25 minutes
Serve hot with or without vanilla ice cream

High Cotton

MP 1. Beach Road
Kitty Hawk, North Carolina

www.highcottonbbq.com   (252) 255-2275

Will Thorp, Owner   Matt Cooper, Chef and Owner
Lori Haynes, Catering Director

I'm not quite sure where the name "High Cotton" came from but in this case it means a good place to enjoy traditional Eastern North Carolina barbeque or an expression of fine living. Consistent temperatures and many hours of smoking with hickory coals is just what are needed to bring that special flavor out. Combine this with a side of Brunswick stew or baked beans and chopped slaw and a glass of sweet tea, and your day is off to a good start, the North Carolina way.

High Cotton has been around since 2003. A collection of many old photos from Edgecomb County and Nash County are displayed on the walls documenting the many ways of cooking barbeque. Open pits were used often as a way of barbequing in the old days.

There are some places you can just count on to be good and High Cotton is one of those, just good old southern food being served with the best barbeque that you'll find anywhere. Combination plates of hand-chopped pork, Matt's famous smoked chicken, southern fried chicken or pulled chicken and beef brisket served with cornsticks with your choice of two sides are just a few of the favorites. Great meals include half and full racks of St. Louis cut ribs, tantalizing Texas style beef brisket and famous Brunswick stew loaded with smoked chicken, potatoes and vegetables. Sandwiches and salads are also a favorite. Fall is always chicken pastry (dumpling) time. Green beans, collards, chicken pot pie along with baked beans, chopped slaw, mashed potatoes are just some of the sides. Be sure and check out the desserts made by Ruth Cooper, especially the chess pies.

High Cotton is well know for their catering service for up to 500 people and their family package deals that feed up to 16. Open daily in season for lunch and dinner. Call for winter hours. Menu available for the Little Piglets. Don't forget those famous High Cotton T-Shirts. Beer available.

Brunswick Stew
(recipe for 250 people)

Bake or smoke 12 whole chickens (better if smoked)
Bake or smoke 3 boston butts (better if smoked)
Use 15 gallon pot or larger
Put 6 #10 cans of diced tomatoes in pot
Add potatoes –10 lb. peeled and cut or diced
Add chicken base—2 ½ cups
Add chef grind pepper (black) ½ cup
Let ingredients cook until tomatoes start to puree (low heat)
Add lima beans (20 lbs.)
Add shoepeg corn (20 lbs.)
Add diced cabbage (8 heads)
Add 1 ½ pictures of water
Let cook until boiling (stir frequently)
Chop boston butts and add to pot
Pull chicken off the bone and add to pot
Cook until boiling (stirring frequently) and chicken is shredding
Very important to stir often. Especially after chicken is added

Takes Approximately 4 hours

Howard's Pub & Raw Bar Restaurant

N.C. Hwy. 12
P.O. Box 670
Ocracoke, North Carolina 27960

The Warner's, Owners   www.howardspub.com   (252) 928-4441

Howard's Pub & Raw Bar Restaurant is the only raw bar on Ocracoke Island. A fun place with great local flavor, no trip to Ocracoke would be complete without a visit to Howard's Pub, home of the famous "Ocracoke Oyster Shooter." You can sit out on the screened –in porch that stretches the entire length of the restaurant or sit inside at one of the wooden tables. Inside you can dance to live music, watch multiple TV's or play games; and if you are not into having fun, you can just sit around and watch everyone else having fun. There's also a large roof top deck for enjoying views of the ocean and sound.

Howard's boasts a huge beer and wine list. This includes over 214 domestic and imported beers. Lunch and dinner items include subs, burgers, sandwiches, snow crab legs, pizzas, soups and salads, munchies and chicken, steaks, lobsters, lots of seafood items from shrimp to oysters and fresh locally caught fish.

The owners are very modest; and if you ask them to boast a little about their restaurant they will say, "We do make a number of items here by hand or from scratch. For example, our chili—but everyone has their own chili recipe; our Italian dressing for subs and salads—but again, not many people need a recipe for salad dressing; our French fries—but that just requires using the right Idaho potatoes and cutting them by hand; our burgers, everybody makes burgers—we use 81% lean beef and shape each one by hand. We are dedicated to using only fresh local vegetables and products when available."

I think they just said all that needs to be said! Howard's is open 365 ½ a year, from lunchtime until the owls go to bed. The Warner's work hard to make your visit to Ocracoke Island a memorable one. Stop in and give them an "Atta Boy" for a job well done. Kids menu available. Live entertainment.

Ocracoke Oyster Shooter

2 to 3 oz. of your favorite beer
1 freshly shucked oyster
Dash of Texas Pete, Tabasco sauce,
   or your preferred hot sauce

Put freshly shucked oyster in a small glass. Add beer. Top with dash of hot sauce and enjoy. Typically, the shooter is consumed in one swallow (although some people prefer to hold the oyster in their mouth a bit to savor), and one or two aren't normally near enough! Real beer lovers say, "The beer helps the oyster go down," but the real oyster lovers say, "The oyster helps the beer go down!"

Hurricane Mo's

Beachside Bar & Grill
120 East Kitty Hawk Rd. M.P. 4
Kitty Hawk, North Carolina

Jeff and Maureen Ashworth, Owners   (252) 255-0215

You'll find this great casual restaurant located right in the heart of Kitty Hawk behind the main post office on the left but steps from the beach road and ocean. Previously located on the top floor of the Pirates Cove ship's store, they relocated in 2005 to their new location at the beach but kept the Pirates Cove location open until the fall of 2007. This restaurant has always been a favorite with the locals and tourist alike. Afternoons from 3 to 5 p.m. brings out the die hard happy hour crowd with those favorite shrimp and wings specials featured.

Hurricane Mo's restaurant is a family oriented atmosphere specializing in Outer Banks and Southern style cuisine. The menu appeals to all tastes. Featured are broiled, fried and steamed seafood platters, ribeye steaks, crab cakes, soups, salads and sandwiches, specialty pastas, appetizers. One of my favorite things on the menu is the CocoMo Mahi —tender dolphin filet marinated in coconut rum and fresh lime juice lightly fried and topped with pineapple chutney and flaked coconut.

Live entertainment is featured on week-ends so call ahead to see who's playing. Full ABC license. A children's menu is available. Open for lunch and dinner daily year round.

Oyster's Mo
(on the halfshell)

1 lb. bacon chopped	1 T. cracked pepper
1 large white onion chopped	1 pint heavy cream
1 large green pepper chopped	1 large tomato, seeded
1 large red pepper chopped	and chopped
¼ lb. cilantro chopped	1 T. Tabasco
2 T. garlic finely chopped	1 cup of fresh grated
1 T. kosher salt	parmesan

1. Sauté bacon until fat is rendered and brown on the edges.
2. Add peppers, onion, cilantro, and seasoning and cook until vegetables are releasing moisture.
3. Add garlic and cook until toasty brown.
4. Add cream and bring to a slow boil, reduce to simmer for 8-10 minutes. Fold in tomato and tobasco.
5. Remove from heat and chill for at least 3 hours.
6. Spoon desired amount on top of fresh shucked oysters on the half-shell. Top with grated parmesan and broil until cheese is slightly brown. Serve immediately.

Rosemary, Corn, and Oyster Cream Stew

1 lb. bacon chopped	¼ c. fresh parsley chopped
2 baking potatoes chopped	2 dry bay leaves
3 cups of yellow corn off the cob	2 T. cracked pepper
¼ lb. butter	2 T. kosher salt
1 large white onion chopped	½ c. flour
6 ribs of celery chopped	1 c. white wine
2 T. fresh rosemary	3 qt. heavy cream
¼ c. garlic chopped	

1. In a large soup pot, sauté bacon until fat is rendered and brown on the edges.
2. Add chopped potatoes and corn and sauté until they begin to stick from starches being released.
3. Add butter, vegetables, seasoning, fresh herbs, bay leaves, and garlic.
4. Sauté very well until moisture from vegetables is nearly evaporated.
5. Add flour until mixture is completely coated and begins to stick to pan, but not burn.
6. Deglaze the pan with white wine and let cook for 2 minutes, stirring well.
7. Add heavy cream and bring to a slow boil.
8. Transfer to double boiler and cook on medium-high heat for 1½ hours.
9. Just before serving, drop in fresh shucked oysters.

I like to serve this around a portion of buttermilk mashed potatoes.

JK's Restaurant

US 158 MP 9
Kill Devil Hills, North Carolina
(252) 441-9555

Timbuck 11 Shopping Center
Corolla, North Carolina
(252) 453-4336

Matt & John Homcy, Owners

The original JK's Restaurant was established in 1984 by JK Norfleet, the founder of wood-fired grilling on the Outer Banks. His philosophy about cooking was to start with an excellent raw product and keep the preparation simple and unadorned as possible. JK's Dry Rub Seasoning recipe originated from a hand-written recipe given to him by a cook on a Texas ranch back in 1971. Once the restaurant opened, the seasoning became the basis for the ribs, chicken and etc.

In 1990, the original JK's restaurant closed due to a fire that destroyed the building that JK Norfleet owned. In the six short years of existence, it had become an Outer Banks institution known around the country. Norfleet never rebuilt because he no longer wanted to be the sole operator of a restaurant. Years later, brothers Matt and John decided to leave the corporate world and head for the Outer Banks. They remembered the dry-rubbed baby back ribs that they once tasted while visiting the area on vacation. They contacted JK and asked to license his recipe and name. They opened JK's Ribs next to a miniature golf course in Kill Devil Hills. In 1998, the brothers decided to move to their now, permanent location.

You will be pleasantly delighted when you're escorted to one of the half dozen three-sided alcoves off the main dining area where each table is covered with a linen tablecloth. Low lighting and candles at each table with jazz playing in the background definitely add a touch of class to your dining experience. The highlight of the evening though is the outstanding cuisine. The specialty is Western Beef steaks aged in-house along with their mesquite-grilled baby-back ribs. A great supporting cast of succulent seafood, tender veal, poultry, and salads are also recommended. It's not often that you find a restaurant with its own skilled in-house butcher but Mac Magruder just happens to be the best and has been with JK's since its original opening.

The wine list is expansive but affordable here. A full service bar is located near the entrance with high cherry wood bar tables for more casual dining. JK's also offers their "JK's Dry Seasoned Rub" for sale. A children's menu is available. Dinner is served nightly in season. Call for winter hours.

JK's Boot-Kicking Grilled Tenderloin with a Red Wine Mustard Caper Sauce

4-5 pounds beef tenderloin, fully trimmed, see note

Serves 6 to 8 for dinner

JK's Marinade

1/3 cup Dijon mustard	2 T. olive oil
2-3 T. red wine vinegar	1 tsp. dried rosemary
2 T.soy sauce	1 tsp. dried thyme
¼ cup dry white wine	salt and pepper to taste
2 cloves minced garlic	

Trim tenderloin and place in a roasting pan. Salt and pepper the meat.
Make marinade: Mix all the ingredients except olive oil and herbs. Pour in olive oil in a slow steady stream; whisk until well-blended. Stir in herbs. Rub the marinade generously over up to 2 tenderloins. Makes ¾ cup.
Refrigerate the meat for at least 8 hours, periodically rubbing the marinade over the meat.
Prepare grill. Place meat over coals, turning the tenderloin over so that it browns on all sides. Cook until it reaches an internal temperature of 120 degrees for medium rare, about 10 to 12 minutes. Remember that meat continues to cook after it's been taken off the fire, so allow time before serving for the meat to rest. Serve alone or for a more special occasion, serve with the Red Wine Mustard Caper Sauce below.
Note: When you buy tenderloin, make sure it's fully trimmed with the silver skin removed. When grilling meat you lose about 20% in the cooking process, so a 4-5 pound tenderloin will become 2 ½ to 3.
(½ pounds once cooked. Figure that into your serving count.)

Red Wine Mustard Caper Sauce

½ cup red wine	2 T. Dijon mustard
1 cup plus 2 T. beef broth, divided	¼ cup small capers,
½ cup heavy cream	rinsed and drained
4 tsp. cornstarch	salt and pepper to taste

In a heavy-bottomed saucepan reduce wine by half. Add 1 cup beef broth and bring to a boil. Add cream and return to a boil. Dissolve cornstarch in remaining 2 tablespoons beef broth. Add to saucepan and boil until slightly thickened, about 3-4 minutes. Stir in mustard, capers and any accumulated juices from meat. Season with salt and pepper. Makes 1 ¼ to 1 ½ cups.

Jason's Restaurant
1134 Irvin Garrish Hwy. NC 12
Ocracoke Island, North Carolina

Jason Wells, Owner/Chef
James Bowen, Owner/Chef

(252)928-3434

Located on the north end of Ocracoke Village, you'll find Jason's to be the perfect place to catch the island spirit with its casual atmosphere, great food, and friendly service. This is definitely a great place to hang out and to meet people. The ambiance is upbeat with a spacious screened porch for those who prefer to sit outside or just sit at the bar and watch the chefs perform their magic. The inside dining room is simple with its plank flooring but very inviting. Locals and visitors alike love this place.

The menu features traditional Outer Banks Seafood, 6 oz. prime tenderloin, chicken, pastas, lasagna, homemade soups and salads, appetizers. Pizzas are the number one seller here, some say it's the best they have ever had. There's also a large variety of sandwiches and subs available. For the hardy appetite, there's the NY strip steak sub with 5 oz. of prime N.Y. strip loin with choice of cheese. Desserts are made fresh daily

You'll find Jason and James along with Wookie busy at work in the kitchen preparing meals. Recipes given below are two that the locals call their favorites. A wide variety of keg beer, domestic, and imports bottles are available along with some nicely priced wines. Carry-out is available for all the menu items. Open for lunch and dinner year round. Call for winter hours.

Clam and Fish Chowder
Serves 8 to 10

1 tablespoon butter	½ lb. butter or margarine, melted
1 onion	2 cups heavy cream
½ bunch celery	½ cup chopped fresh parsley
1 tablespoon thyme	
2 tablespoons Old Bay seasoning	
1 cup crumbled cooked bacon	
4 cups fresh shucked clams, chopped, including liquid, (can use frozen or canned clams with liquid)	

10 to 12 cups of clam broth or fish stock
3 lbs. potatoes cubed
2 lbs. cubed mild fish such as mahi-mahi, drum or salmon
In large stockpot, sauté in butter, onion, celery, thyme, Old Bay, and
bacon. Add clams and broth. Bring to a boil and then add potatoes.
Cook until potatoes are tender. Add remaining seafood. In a small
saucepan combine butter and flour to make roux, cooking on low
for a couple of minutes. Whisk roux into soup stirring until slightly
thickened. Add cream, salt, pepper, and Tabasco to taste. Remove
from heat, stir in parsley and serve.

Tiramisu

Dessert serves 12 to 16

3 packages ladyfingers or sponge cake cut into fingers
12 eggs separated
2 ½ cups sugar

1 ½ lb. mascarpone cheese (can substitute 1 lb. cream cheese) make
 sure its room temperature.
½ cup sour cream
4 tablespoons whipping cream
Beat cheese, sour cream, whipping cream all together

½ cup kahlua
½ cup strong coffee
3 cups whipping cream
unsweetened cocoa powder
chocolate curls if desired

Beat together *egg yolks* and sugar. Place in double boiler and cook
whisking constantly until thick and pale about 3 to 4 minutes. Remove
from heat. Beat yolks/sugar mixture into cheese. In a separate bowl
beat 1 cup *egg whites* until stiff. Fold into custard. In another bowl
beat whipping cream until stiff and fold gently into custard.
To assemble: In a large rectangular dish or individual serving bowls
place a layer of ladyfingers. Brush with kahlua/coffee mixture. Spoon
custard over. Layer again with kahlua/coffee and more custard. Sift
cocoa powder over all and garnish with chocolate curls if desired.

Jolly Roger Pub & Marina

410 Irvin Garrish Hwy.
Ocracoke Village
Ocracoke, North Carolina

Peggy Wrobleski, Owner

(252) 928-3703

Sergio Mendoza, Chef

There's definitely not a bad seat to be found in this outside pub located on picturesque Silver Lake Harbor. This is the first place I head for when arriving on Ocracoke Island just so I can take in all the scenery and enjoy some really great food in a very casual atmosphere. Nothing fancy here, just pull up one of those plastic chairs and have a seat and watch Cap. John Ferrars coming in on the boat "Fish Tale" or watch fish being unloaded from boats next door at the Ocracoke Fish Company.

The menu offers appetizers, soups, salads, landlubber and sea sandwiches, seafood and chicken baskets, south of the border favorites and desserts. There are always daily specials, but if you're looking for that homemade crab cake sandwich, local seafood, then you're at the right place. Kate Plyler was my waitress on this last trip, she was superior.

This restaurant is part of the Marina Hotel located just across the street and has been in business for the last 18 years. Beer and wine are available. A kid's treasure chest menu is available. Open daily from spring thru fall season serving lunch and dinner. Live entertainment at sunset.

Crab & Corn Chowder

2	cups fresh corn or frozen (thawed)	¼	cup red pepper, diced
1½	cups potatoes cut into cubes	1	cup half and half cream
4	tsp. butter	½	tsp. red hot pepper flakes
¼	cup carrots, cubed	½	tsp. paprika
1½	cups celery, sliced	½	T. seafood base
2	cups fish broth **or**	¼	tsp. chili powder
	(1 cup bottled clam juice and 1 cup water)		
2	cups crab meat		
	Salt and fresh ground pepper		
1½	cups chopped onions		

Heat the butter in a large skillet. Add the onions, carrots, red pepper, celery and potatoes. Stir over a medium heat until the onions are wilted. Heat the half and half and add the potato mixture with the fish broth, salt and pepper and hop pepper flakes. Add the corn and _half_ of the crab meat and stir. Simmer for 6 to 8 minutes until the potatoes are tender, add rest of crab meat, and stir gently. Heat thoroughly and serve.

Jolly Roger Restaurant

1836 Virginia Dare Trail (Beach Road). MP 6 ¾
Kill Devil Hills, North Carolina

Carol Ann Angelos, Owner

Cory Schleicher, Executive Chef, CEC

(252) 441-6530

www.jollyrogerobx.com

This cozy white cottage with the big glass bubble is known as the "Jolly Roger." It sits across the road from the ocean and has been catering to locals and tourists since 1972. It's a comfortable, casual place where you just might run into someone you least expect to see. It's is the oldest Italian restaurant on the beach and is known for serving great Italian food and huge portions.

This restaurant is anything but fancy, a combination of tacky, pirate themed, Christmas balls & lights and anything else that can be glued or hung from the ceilings and walls. It's definitely a place you won't forget. A new second floor outside deck was just added in 2013 for guest to enjoy ocean views while waiting to be seated,

Jolly Roger's Executive Chef Cory Schleicher is a French Italian trained chef and a graduate of Newbury College in Boston. He was a chef at the famous La Scalas restaurant in Boston and later at the Oceanfront Trellis and the Waterfront Trellis on the Outer Banks. He also can be seen on the Hampton Roads Television show in Virginia once a month. Be sure and check out Chef Cory's featured menu of the day which might include Shrimp & Scallops alla Vodka sautéed with garlic and Roma tomatoes in a vodka cream sauce with crimini mushrooms & penne pasta. Oh, so good.

Guests enjoy great Italian food, good old-fashioned breakfasts, diner type lunches and fresh seafood, steaks, pasta and prime rib, featured at dinner. Friday night is Prime Rib night and just happens to be my favorite place for prime rib. Open year-round for breakfast, lunch, dinner. There is entertainment and trivia games nightly in the lounge and plenty room for dancing. Every night features the Allen Ross Karaoke Road Show, one of the best in the country. A full late night menu is available until 1 a.m.

Be sure and check out their large bar with TV's. This is a poplar bar for night time entertainment. Open year-round for breakfast, lunch, dinner. Full ABC license.

Blackened Chicken Carbonara
(Serves 4)

4 each butterfly chicken breasts
6 tablespoons blackening spice
2 tablespoons olive oil
2 tablespoons chopped garlic
¼ cup shaved & julienned prosciutto
10 each button mushrooms-sliced
½ cup frozen peas
¼ cup white wine

2 cups heavy cream
½ cup grated parmesan
4 cups frozen tri-color-cheese tortellini
salt & pepper to taste
fresh parmesan & parsley-for garnish

Dredge chicken in blackening spice & sear in ½ of the oil on both sides. Finish in oven if necessary. Heat remaining oil in a large sauté pan. Add garlic, prosciutto & mushrooms and sauté till garlic is slightly browned. Add frozen peas & tortellini then deglaze with white wine. Add heavy cream & bring to a boil, lower heat & simmer for 3-5 minutes. Add grated parmesan & season with salt & pepper. Garnish with fresh shaved parmesan & chopped parsley.

Stuffed Flounder

2 ea. 5 to 7 oz. flounder fillets
3 oz. butter
Juice of 1 lemon
1 T. roasted garlic pepper
1 oz. white wine
Salt and pepper to taste
2 oz lump crabmeat

2 oz. small shrimp, peeled
1 oz. mayonnaise
1 oz. bread crumbs
6 oz. heavy cream
2 oz. tomato sauce
1 tsp. each, chopped basil & parsley

To make stuffing: Combine the crabmeat, shrimp, mayonnaise, and bread crumbs.

To make sauce: Mix together the heavy cream, tomato sauce, basil and parsley. Heat and reduce until thickened.

Place 1 of the flounder fillets, skin side down on a greased sizzle plate. Place the filling in the center of the fillet. Cut a slit down the center of the other fillet, being careful not to cut so far as to separate the fillet. Place this fillet over the top of the stuffing and spread apart to partly expose the stuffing. Sprinkle the lemon juice, white wine, salt and pepper, and roasted garlic pepper seasoning over the stuffed flounder. Bake in a preheated 350-degree oven for 15 to 20 minutes. Remove from oven, top with the sauce and serve. Be sure to remind everyone that the platter is hot!

Kelly's

Outer Banks Restaurant & Tavern
US 158 Bypass MP 10
Nags Head, North Carolina 27959

Mike Kelly, Owner   (252) 441-4116

Jeff Wasnesky, Executive Chef   Becky Miller, Pastry Chef

Kelly's is one of the most popular restaurants on the Outer Banks and considered to be a tradition among many visitors that return year after year. Owner Mike Kelly is always present greeting guest and giving special attention to every detail of service. When you visit Kelly's, you'll dine amongst the largest collection of Outer Banks memorabilia and artifacts to be found anywhere. The menu offers the freshest selections from the sea, as well as tender beef, veal and delicate pasta. Homemade breads, including sweet potato biscuits are served with all meals. The 2010 Taste of The Beach People's Choice Award for best dessert was won by Kelly's Restaurant. They also received awards for 1st Place for Best Outer Banks Cuisine and 3rd Place in Best Overall.

The raw bar offers oysters, clams, crab legs, shrimp. Great live entertainment can be found at Kelly's Tavern nightly starting at 10 PM when it becomes a fun-loving party place. The Tavern has a large two story addition with the largest dance floor on the Outer Banks, an upstairs bar, and a large seating area overlooking the dance floor.

This large casual restaurant is a busy place in season. Open year round, dinner is served nightly. Full catering service available.

Sweet Potato and Crab Stuffed Shrimp with Saffron Aioli

Stuffing:
1 doz. day old sweet potato biscuits, grated fine to medium
1 red bell pepper, small dice
1 green bell pepper, small dice
1 red onion, small dice
2 T. fresh cilantro
1 cup clarified butter
½ lb. jumbo lump crabmeat

salt and pepper to taste

Stuffing: mix all ingredients together except the butter. Add butter slowly to the mix until it binds together (may not take full cup of butter)

Saffron Aioli:

1 cup mayonnaise
pinch saffron (steep in small amount of hot water)

Thoroughly mix mayonnaise and saffron until mayo has a nice bright yellow appearance.

2 doz. shrimp, preferably 16/20 count peeled, deveined and butter flied

<u>*Cooking Directions:*</u> Preheat oven to 350 degrees, roll stuffing into small to medium balls. Sit balls atop shrimp w/tails curled up. Place on greased cookie sheet. Bake for 10 minutes or until shrimp are pink. Place a dab of aioli on top of each shrimp

Sweet Potato Biscuits

1 lb. cooked sweet potatoes
1 cup light brown sugar
¼ cup water
2 ¼ cup bisquick

Cool and peel sweet potatoes, mix together sweet potatoes, brown sugar, bisquick, and water. Combine thoroughly (the mixture will be moister than regular biscuits.) flour table, roll biscuit mix to ½" thickness. Cut with 2 ½ inch cutter. Place on greased sheet pan, bake in preheated 350 degree oven for 16-18 minutes. The moist mixture does not allow the biscuits to rise a great deal. A mindful eye should be kept on the biscuits so they do not over cook.

Kill Devil Grill

2008 S. Virginia Dare Trail (Beach Rd.) MP 9 ¾
Kill Devil Hills, North Carolina

Bill Tucker, Owner, Chef   (252) 449-8181

The original former owner's interest in Vintage diners led to the purchase of this 1939 Kullman diner in Richmond, Virginia. Once restored to its former glory, it was moved to its present site in 1996 to serve as the former Millie's restaurant. Today, this Landmark Diner Bar is one of only six diners listed in the National Registry of Historic Buildings in this country. Classic individual Seeburgs are found at each booth and on the counter. Chrome tables and old rock and rhythm & blues LPs frame the walls and give the Kill Devil Grill a classy look. Tongue-and-groove ceiling also add a special touch.

Food at the Kill Devil Grill is creative, distinctive and delicious. They use only the freshest local seafood and ingredients purchased daily. Meals are prepared from scratch daily; The dinner menu offers both light fare or full blown entrees such as crab cakes, shrimp, BBQ ribs and chicken, ribeye steaks served with homemade mashed potatoes and grilled mushrooms, salads, wood roasted chicken. Be sure and check out the blue plate special and fresh fish of the day on the chalkboard. Lunch menu items include the catfish reuben sandwich, burgers, grilled chicken sandwich, Southern fried chicken, salads, and big plate dinners.

The desserts are wonderful and best of all, home made. The Key Lime pie just happens to be my favorite served with whip cream and a strawberry sauce. The Virginia Pilot newspaper" Taste Test, the best of 2007" voted this restaurants key lime pie recipe the best in the entire area of coastal Virginia and North Carolina.

A children's menu is available. Open year-round with ABC license and a full bar. Sunday brunch is also served in season from 11:00-3:00. Carry-out is available. Call for winter hours.

Hawaiian Steak Marinade

Shelf life: 4 days
Sensitivity: Mix dry spices until lump free, marinade may be used (1) time only
Tools: Quart & cup measuring containers, large stainless steel bowl; wire whip, 1 gallon Cambro containers with lids.

1	pint Soy Sauce
1 ½	cups rice vinegar
¾	cup ketchup
1 1/3	tablespoons Paprika
2	tablespoons garlic powder
2	tablespoons fresh minced garlic
24	ounces pineapple juice
1	ounce pureed ginger root, peeled

1. Place ketchup in a large stainless steel bowl. Add paprika, garlic powder, and minced garlic. Whip until lump free
2. Add Soy sauce and rice vinegar; blend well. Transfer to 1 gallon Cambro containers. Cover, label, date and refrigerate,
3. Marinade may be used one time only, and then thrown away.

Serves 4

Kimball's Kitchen
The Sanderling Resort & Spa
Duck, North Carolina

www.thesanderling-resort.com   (252) 261-8419

John Lawrence, Chef de Cuisine   Phil Bay, Sous Chef

The Sanderling Inn Resort & Spa has added another fine dining restaurant to its nationally acclaimed world class resort. Kimball's Kitchen, formally, The Left Bank, will offer steak and seafood entrees with traditional side dishes and an extensive raw oyster selection. A 60-seat fine dining restaurant, is truly one of first class in every respect. The restaurant offers spectacular views of the Currituck Sound from every seat. A serene environment has been created on the interior for the enjoyment of the finest cuisine on the Outer Banks and the region. The exterior of the building is intended to be a sculptural object that uses the traditional materials and forms of the region in new ways to complement the surroundings. Even the exterior of the building at one end displays the logo "Bird in Flight."

The dining room consists of a mix of free-standing tables and leather banquettes. Only the finest china, silver flatware and crystal are used here. The European open kitchen design with an island stove and granite counter is open to the dining area below where diners can watch as the food is prepared.

The menu features non-pretentious, colorful and flavorful healthy cuisine. The food style is a blend of contemporary American with the technique and traditions of the French culinary arts. Their mission is to serve the bounty of local farmers and fisherman with an emphasis on using Sustainable, Organic, Artisanal and local ingredients, a concept they refer to as S.O.A.L. This fine dining restaurant features grass-fed prime steaks, numerous varieties of local oysters and the classic seafood tower and a wine and champagne list that is superb. Nightly specials are offered.

Kimball's Kitchen is a multiple Wine Spectator Award of Excellence winner and has received the coveted AAA Four Diamond award since its opening in 2003. Stop by The Blond Onyx Bar after 5:p.m. for a late afternoon cocktail or glass of wine while enjoying the breathtaking sunsets over

the Currituck Sound and say hello to the bartender, Frank Poorman, or drop in after dinner (no reservations required) and indulge in fabulous desserts, artisanal cheeses, vintage ports and fine cordials.   The restaurant is open Tuesday through Saturday from May –October with live entertainment on Saturday evenings. Kimball's Kitchen can accommodate large parties, rehearsal dinners and events for up to 60 people. Children are welcome and are served smaller portions of the standard menu at half price.
Reservations recommended for dinner.

Fresh Ricotta Dumplings
Serves 4

Ingredients:
12 oz Ricotta Fresca-well drained in a fine mesh strainer
2 oz Parmesan Reggiano-finely grated
1/3 cup Bread Crumbs-fine
1 Large Egg-lightly beaten
2 Tbsp Parsley-chopped
1 Tbsp Thyme-picked and chopped
3 Tbsp Kosher Salt

Method:

Bring a large pot with 4 quarts of water to a boil,. Mix the Ricotta, Parmesan, and egg together until just combined. Add the Breadcrumbs, Parsley, Thyme and 1 tablespoon of the Salt to the cheese and egg mixture and stir to combine. Use a heaping tablespoon to measure the size of the dumplings. Roll the dumplings in your hands to form a ball set aside and repeat with the remaining mixture. When the water is at a boil add the remaining 2 Tbsp of kosher salt and return to a boil. Add the dumplings to the water and turn the heat down to a simmer, cook the dumplings until they float to the surface. Serve with your favorite pasta sauce. Enjoy

Lifesaving Station Restaurant

NO.5 Bar & Lounge at the Sanderling Inn Resort
1461 Duck Road, N.C. Hwy. 12
Duck, North Carolina

Tim Nelson, Chef de Cuisine   (252) 449-6654
Jeffery Russell, Executive Chef

The first structure on this stretch of sand was built in 1874 but was replaced in 1899 with the Caffey's Inlet U.S. Lifesaving Station NO.5 and was manned by brave souls to save shipwrecked seafarers. Today, that station houses what has become known as Lifesaving Station Restaurant, a part of the world famous Sanderling Inn Resort. The restaurant's dining room, a mixture of polished wood furnishings and nautical mementos, was once the station's boathouse. Throughout the restaurant are reminders of another era in time, an enormous bell for fog warnings, a Lyle gun, even a large ship's compass and a ship's wheel in the NO.5 Bar.

Lifesaving Station Restaurant is one of the Outer Bank's most acclaimed restaurants serving Southern Regional Cuisine for breakfast, lunch and dinner. The menu of imaginatively prepared dishes, including fresh seafood specialties, local grown vegetables, certified Angus beef, is complemented by an extensive selection of domestic and imported wines. The Wine Spectator Magazine has honored this restaurant with its Award of Excellence since 1998. During holidays throughout the year, a three-course Sunday brunch is served and known as the best on the beach. The lunch menu features soups, salads, sandwiches, and other daily specials. Dinner entrees include Roasted Rainbow Trout stuffed with Brie, sweet peppers and lump crabmeat, with cream corn sauce over wild rice.

The second floor of the restaurant houses the NO.5 Bar and Lounge, an intimate gathering place for guests. Lite Fare is available in the Bar until 10:00 p.m. nightly. Reservations are strongly encouraged for dinner in season. The restaurant is opened year-round. A child's menu is available.

Shrimp, Corn, and Crab Chowder

4 slices bacon
6 cups chicken stock or broth
½ lemon, pits removed
2 lbs. fresh shrimp
2 T. butter
1 medium onion, minced
2 celery ribs, minced
2 T. minced green bell pepper
2 cups frozen corn, thawed

Salt, freshly ground pepper
Tabasco
1 cup heavy cream
2 small carrots,
  (sliced paper thin)
½ red bell pepper,
  (cut into very small cubes)
3 oz. Sautéed Lump Crab

Fry the bacon till crisp, drain on paper towels, pour off all but 2 tablespoons of grease and crumble the bacon. In a large saucepan, combine one-half the chicken stock, the lemon half (squeezed), and the shrimp. Bring to a boil, remove from heat, cover and let stand 3 minutes. Drain the shrimp in a colander, pouring the hot stock into another large, heavy saucepan. Discard the lemon half. When cool enough to handle, shell and devein the shrimp. Reserve 12 shrimp, put remainder of the shrimp though a blender or food processor with the remaining stock.

In a skillet, heat the reserved bacon grease and butter, add the onion, celery and green pepper, and saute over low heat about 3 minutes or till vegetables are soft. Add the corn to the shrimp mixture and cook over moderate heat for 2 minutes, stirring. Add the sauteed vegetables to the mixture, stir, bring to a brisk boil, reduce heat and cook 2 minutes.

Remove from the heat, add seasonings to taste, cover and let stand 30 minutes. When ready to serve, bring chowder almost to a boil, stir in heavy cream, carrots, and red pepper cubes, and taste for seasoning. Ladle the chowder into heated soup plates and garnish each portion with crabmeat plus a sprinkling of crumbled bacon. Serves 6

Lucky 12 Tavern

3308 S. Virginia Dare Trail,   MP 11.5
Nags Head, N.C.

Mark Ballog, Owner   www.lucky12tavern.com   (252) 255-5825

Don't miss the chance to have lunch or dinner at this favorite spot on the beach road. Locals, tourists, college kids, sports fans, bikers and everyone in between love to hang out here. It's a fun place offering affordable dining featuring local seafood, burgers, pasta, soups & salads, sandwiches, stone oven specialty pizzas and wings. There's 20 beers on draft, another 100 by the bottle or can. If beer isn't your thing, then try their selections of wines, specialty drinks or one of the 40 martini recipes offered.

This restaurant is located in the former Ball Grocery store that served the local community in the 70's. In 2006 Mark purchased this location to open his own restaurant, a big dream he had from the early age of four on. Somewhere along the way he acquired a love for old antique gas pumps, antique Coca'Cola machines, vintage signs and advertising memorabilia which are displayed throughout this unique restaurant.

Fresh seafood is purchased locally with all soups, salad dressings, handmade burgers (no frozen burgers here) and New York style pizzas baked in special ovens made in –house. For lunch, try the fried fish sandwich or the tavern burger. Another favorite is the Philly cheesesteak sandwich. Dinner choices include fried seafood combos, their famous crabcakes, shrimp and oysters, steaks and pasta of the day.

Lucky 12 turns into a bar atmosphere after 10:00 p.m. and closes at 2:00:a.m. The tavern has a large red top bar and another outside patio bar for just kicking back with a beer and enjoying life on the OBX. If you're here to watch a big game, no problem with 16 TV's available. If you just want to shoot a game of pool and have a PBR, then you definitely are in the right place for fun.

Open year round for lunch and dinner.

The Spicy Remoulade recipe below serves 25-30 people. It's a great recipe for party or home use. Goes well with oysters, fish and seafood.

Spicy Remoulade

1 cup celery (rough cut)
1 cup Yellow onion (peeled & cut into quarters)
1 cup white vinegar
1 oz. capers
½ TBSP minced garlic
4 cups Mayo
½ TBSP Kosher salt
½ TBSP Black Pepper
1 Tsp. cayenne Pepper
4 TBSP coarse ground mustard
¼ Tsp Cumin
¼ Tsp Coriander

1.) Put first 5 ingredients in robo coupe and chop until smooth
2.) Mix remaining ingredients in large mixing bowl and add the combined first 5 ingredients

Chipotle BBQ Sauce

½ cup diced banana Peppers
1 cup fine diced yellow onion
¼ cup olive oil
2 TBSP chopped garlic
1 #10 can ketchup
1 TBSP kosher salt
1 TBSP pepper
2 cups brown sugar
½ cup white vinegar
¼ cup molasses
1 can chipotle peppers (16oz)

1.) Saute first 4 ingredients until onions are translucent
2.) Add remaining ingredients except chipotle peppers, cook for approximately 1 hour then add chipotle peppers & Burrmix until smooth

Mako Mike's

1630 N. Croatan Hwy. Route 158 MP 7
Kill Devil Hills, North Carolina

Frank Gajar, Mike Kelly, Owners   (252) 480-1919

Fred Virgil, Executive Chef   Bill Martin, General Manager

It's easy to spot this luscious-colored restaurant with its gigantic carved shark on the front and lots of shark tails protruding out of the lawn. It's even more decorative inside with sharks peering at diners from almost every angle of the unique three level dining areas. There's even a 200-gallon aquarium in the waiting area.

It's the good food, moderate prices, friendly staff that keep diners returning to this establishment. Traditional and Cajun flavored food, fresh local seafood, salads, pastas, wood oven pizzas, meat dishes and daily specials are available. Don't forget to visit their gift shop or have a cocktail in the Enchanted Octopus Lounge. Of all of the delicious homemade desserts, a favorite of the customer's is the Chocolate Passion Cake.

Open year round. Be sure and ask about the nightly specials. There's also a shark trivia menu for the kids. Large groups welcome. Full ABC license.

Chocolate Passion Cake

16 oz. semi-sweet chocolate chips	1 ½ c. sugar
8 oz. butter, salted	1 c. walnuts or pecans
1 c. cocoa powder	Softened butter & flour
7 eggs	for 10" springform pan

Rub inside of springform pan with butter and lightly coat with flour; tap out excess flour. Wrap outside of springform pan with foil. Melt chocolate and butter in metal bowl over double-boiler and stir until smooth. Add cocoa powder and stir mixture with a whisk until blended; approximately 5 minutes. Set mixture aside.

In another metal bowl, combine eggs and sugar, and warm over double-boiler. Stir constantly until mixture is 110 degrees or lukewarm (2-3 minutes). Pour mixture into mixing bowl of electric mixer and using the whisk attachment, whip until tripled in volume. Fold this mixture into chocolate mixture along with the nuts using a rubber spatula, (do not mix). Pour mixture into springform pan. Place springform pan into another pan which has ½ inch of hot water. Bake for 40-45 minutes at 350 degrees. Remove from oven and cool. Remove springform pan from cake. Slice and serve with sweetened whipped cream.

Metropolis Tapas Restaurant

520 Old Stoney Rd.
Corolla, North Carolina

Matt Kristof, Owner

Mark Anthony, Owner, Executive Chef

(252) 453-6167

www.metropolisobx.com

This restaurant gets its name from the ship "Metropolis" that ran aground in 1878 just off the shores of the Outer Banks and sank near Corolla. When the original owners opened this restaurant in 2002, tapas as a dining style was a new concept to the country, let alone our small island community. In the early days Mark and Matt were regular customers and eventually came to work for the restaurant. Quickly realizing the unique fit M&M amicably bought the business in 2007.

The two young business owners complement each other. Each have a way of making their customers feel like they are special, and that they are personally being attended to by the owners. Mark runs the kitchen and is quickly gaining recognition as a renowned chef for his laid back, creative and contemporary style. He comes out of the kitchen and on most nights personally explains the specials and menu items of note to new and regular customers alike. Matt runs the bar and is unrivaled in his knowledge of the drinks the bar has to offer.

The food and drink available mirror the interior of this hotspot, urban and upscale but with a casual; all are welcome, beach vibe. Mark brings in only the finest local, seasonal, exotic and internationally prized ingredients. Having assembled a core of uniquely talented restaurant professionals the food offered pushes the envelope of what a restaurant can be. In a beach with quite limited ethnic opportunity as far as dinner out, Metropolis prides itself on offering dishes from as many different cultures as possible. On any given night one is sure to find multiple Asian dishes, whether they are Japanese, Chinese or Thai. As well, Italian, Mediterranean, and classical European dishes are standard. There is no shortage of Southwestern and Mexican fare and of course, the regional "New Southern" and "Metrostyle" offerings breathe new life into old ideas and showcase the talents and playful side of the kitchen staff.

The same attention to quality and detail carries over into the front of the house in the beverage service. One will find 25 single malt scotches and small batch bourbons, over 80 hand built martinis featuring local fresh fruits and imaginative combinations. The wine list is eclectic and offers limited production and boutique wines as well as rare gems that Mark and Matt have dug up over the years. Open year round for dinner and during summer season from 5 p.m till 2.a.m. Call about private parties, catering and wedding functions.

"Metrostyle" Macaroni & Cheese

(4 servings)

8 oz. potato gnocchi (available at grocery or specialty store)
4 oz. chorizo (2 links, mild or spicy as per taste)
4 oz. shredded Vermont cheddar
3 scallions, green part only, chopped
20 grape tomatoes, halved
2 Tbsp. butter
1 cup heavy cream
Salt & Pepper
White Truffle Oil

Garlic & Parmesan Breadcrumbs (recipe to follow)

For the breadcrumbs you will need:
1/2 cup panko breadcrumbs
2 Tbsp. Extra Virgin Olive Oil
2 tsp. minced fresh garlic
2 Tbsp. finely grated parmesan cheese
Salt

Toast garlic in E.V.O.O. until light brown on medium-low heat
Add Panko crumbs and toss until evenly coated with garlic and oil
while still on heat add parmesan and toast lightly add salt, spread out
on wax paper to cool.

For the Macaroni & Cheese: You will need a pot with 2 quarts of
slowly boiling water, a large high sided sauté pan, a strainer.
cook chorizo in water for 4 minutes, cool, remove casing
melt butter in sauté pan on medium heat, break up cooked chorizo in
butter and brown lightly in sauté pan, add heavy cream, stir
drop gnocchi in water, when floating (roughly 2 minutes) strain and
discard water, add gnocchi to chorizo and cream mixture add tomato
and scallion, stir, add cheddar, stir until uniformly melted, add salt and
pepper to taste, top with a drizzle of white truffle oil and with garlic-
parmesan breadcrumbs. ENJOY!

Mike Dianna's Grill Room

777 Sunset Blvd. Timbuck II Shops
Corolla, North Carolina

Mike and Lindsey Dianna, Owners   (252) 453-4336
Chris Miller, Chef   www.grillroomobx.com
Meghann Cole, General Manager

Tucked away in the far corner of Timbuck II shopping center lies a restaurant serving great food with great views of the Currituck Sound to boot. Mike Dianna arrived on the Outer Banks in 1995 with the thoughts of owning his own restaurant one day, a childhood dream since the age of fourteen. He took over as manager of JK's in Corolla in 1999 and later purchased that location turning it into the present "Grill Room." Part of the restaurants appeal is Mike and Lindsey's dedication to making the restaurant feel as if it's an extension of their own home, therefore making every guest feel welcome.

The large menu selection changes daily and features something for everyone from USDA prime beef (specialty of the house), fresh fish, Italian favorites, healthy selections, soups & salads, appetizers. The steaks here are hand selected and cut in house. An excellent beginning to any meal is the fried oysters that just happen to be a favorite. Another house favorite is Mike's famous crab cakes and if you like Italian, well, you just have to try Joan's (Mike's mom) recipe for baked ziti. Oh, lets not forget dessert, they have a mesquite grilled banana split that is made by grilling the bananas over mesquite coals and topping off with vanilla and chocolate ice creams, fresh strawberries, chocolate sauce, and whipped cream.

The "Grill Room" was awarded the "Wine Spectator Award of Excellence" for 2005 offering more than 200 wines and specialty cocktails. Catering is offered both inside and outside restaurant for any size party.

A kids menu is available for those little ones. Come and enjoy live music on the decks and see what this restaurant is all about. Reservations highly recommended in season. Open year round. Call for winter hours.

Grill Room Seafood Chowder
Serves 4-8 people

1   qt. half and half
½   qt. heavy cream
1   `qt. chicken stock
¼   cup lobster base
2/3 cup carrot, small dice

2/3 cup celery, small dice
1 cup yellow onion, small dice
½ T. salt
½ T. pepper
3 oz. butter
3 oz. flour
½ cup red bell pepper, fresh, small diced
1 cup corn
2 cups potatoes, diced
½ cup parsley
½ cup dry sherry
¼ lb. clam meat
¾ lb. fish and shellfish (anything will work)

In a tall stock pot, heat first 4 ingredients on medium heat and bring to
a simmer. Sauté, carrot, celery and onion with salt and pepper in butter
until onion is transparent. Mix in flour to make roux. Slowly whisk
roux into liquid, very hot, but not quite simmering, stirring the whole
time. Steam fish and shellfish. Add potatoes, corn and red pepper,
allow to simmer over low heat---stir often to prevent scorching. Add
seafood and clams with their juices while hot. Add sherry and parsley
and simmer for 5 more minutes. Serve warm

Millers Seafood & Steak House

1520 S. Virginia Dare Trail (Beach Rd)   MP 9 ½
Nags Head, North Carolina

Brian Beth Miller, Owners   (252) 441-7674

Millers Seafood and Steak House is a family owned and operated restaurant dating back almost 30 years when Eddie and Lou Miller ran the restaurant, now owned by their son Brian and wife Beth.. The tradition of southern hospitality is still being carried on by this next generation. Sensational seafood at family prices and the highest quality NC seafood and Angus beef are served to their customers and it's been that way since 1978.

A large menu is available with "All You Can Eat" items such as clam strips, ocean trout, and popcorn shrimp; specializing in fresh seafood and steaks. The Surf and Turf combos are wonderful. You can get just about any type of seafood here including soft-shell crabs. Appetizers, salads, sandwiches are also available. If you have room left, try one of the wonderful homemade desserts

Millers is still serving a full breakfast menu featuring their homemade sausage gravy, creamed chipped beef, steak and eggs, omelettes country ham and so much more. Open for breakfast from 7 a.m. till 12 p.m. and dinner from March to late fall. Full ABC permits serving your favorite mixed beverages. Children's menu

Outer Banks Stuffed Flounder

½ c. mayonnaise
¼ c. Dijon mustard
1 lb. fresh lump crabmeat
pinch lemon pepper
pinch cayenne pepper

pinch garlic salt
2 T. bread crumbs
12-5 oz. skinless boneless
    flounder fillets

Mix mayonnaise, mustard, lemon pepper, cayenne pepper, garlic salt and bread crumbs in mixing bowl; add crabmeat (be sure to remove any shell) and gently fold into mixture.

Slice 6 of the flounder fillets in half; lay the other 6 flounder fillets about 2 inches apart from each other on a buttered baking pan.

Spoon 3 oz. crab mix on top of flounder fillets; place the sliced fillets on the top of the stuffed fillets and brush lightly with melted butter. Broil in oven approximately 15 minutes. Yields 6 servings.

Miller's Waterfront Restaurant

6916 S. Croatan Hwy. (MP 16)
Nags Head, North Carolina 27959

millerswaterfront.com   (252) 441-6151

Bryan and Whitney Miller Wilson, Owners, Operators

Miller's might not have oceanfront views but they definitely have the most spectacular   views of the Roanoke Sound and that glorious sunset. The restaurant has a back wall consisting entirely of windows, allowing each and every table an unobstructed water view. During the day, kiteboarders and windsurfers offer plenty of entertainment, while in the evening Mother Nature shows off her skills with the most colorful sunsets to be found.

Miller's Restaurant has been owned and operated by the Miller family since 1982. Eddie and Lou Miller founded the restaurant and have now retired with Whitney (daughter) and Bryan now carrying on the family tradition. The restaurant, often referred to as "Sunset Central" has one of the largest menus on the beach with something for everyone.

Bryan stays busy getting the freshest seafood catch possible and making sure his lunch and dinner specials are the best possible. Their two most popular menu items are the "House Specially Fish Sandwich" which consists of fresh fried grouper topped with fried onion strings and house tarter on crusty ciabatta bread for lunch, and their homemade jumbo lump crab cakes, known as the "House Favorite" for dinner. Miller's makes the best hush puppies I've ever eaten, once you try one, you'll be asking for more.

Miller's restaurant is a casual place with rustic charm. Be sure and take a stroll out on the pier and enjoy the pelicans and herons diving for their meal of the day or that windsurfer trying to get that last minute of surfing in before sunset.

Open for lunch and dinner from March thru October. ABC license. Children's menu

Parmesan and Crab Encrusted Red Snapper
with a Roasted Red Pepper Remoulade

4   6 to 8 oz. filets of Red Snapper (Flounder, Grouper, or Tilapia

Crust
1 cup Panko breadcrumbs (Japanese style)
1 cup grated parmesan cheese
1 lb. jumbo lump crab meat
3 tbsp melted butter
3 tbsp olive oil
1 tsp. tarragon vine

Red Pepper Remoulade
½ cup mayonnaise
1 tbsp capers
1 tbsp pickles
1 tbsp tarragon
2 tsp. minced shallots
1 tsp. Dijon mustard
3 roasted red peppers
(from a can or fire
roasted, skin removed)

Crust: combine all ingredients and mix well by hand

Remoulade: Combine all ingredients in blender and mix until smooth, transfer to a squeeze bottle (remaining sauce will be good for up to two weeks in refrigeration)

Place the filets skin side down on greased baking sheet. Add a thin layer of panko and crab crust. Bake at 400 degrees (preheated) for approximately 8 minutes. Remove from oven place filets on plate and paint the remoulade (with the squeeze bottle) over top of filet. Enjoy!!

Mulligan's Raw Bar & Grille

4005 S. Croatan Hwy. M.P. 13
Nags Head, North Carolina

Gus Zinovis Owner, Shannon Moody, Owner   (252) 480-2000

This warm friendly eatery has been a big hit with locals and tourist since it originally opened on the beach road in 1992. In 2006, a move was in store to a much larger location, the former Bad Barracuda's site just across from Jockey Ridge state park. Definitely a great place to go and meet friends, watch a Sunday football game at the L-shaped bar on the upper level or enjoying a meal while viewing the ocean to the east and Jockey Ridge to the west. The main dining rooms are located on the first floor with a small bar offering views of Jockey Ridge.

Mulligan's was voted Best Burger on the Beach for 6 years running featuring 17 different burgers with burger specials daily.   Soups and salads and a variety of sandwiches, subs, wraps, seafood, steaks and gourmet pizzas are found on the menu. Dinner entrees include great seafood platters, cooked to order and served with fries and homemade coleslaw. They are increasingly becoming renowned for their fresh local seafood dishes. Make sure and check out the daily specials of raw and steamed seafood including buckets of steamed clams. Oh, I forgot to mention the extremely popular shrimp, crab & parmesan dip found on the appetizer list, it's so good.

All desserts are homemade. Try the Key West lime pie or the cheesecake of the day, how about the hot fudge cake made with a warm brownie, ice cream, lots of hot fudge and whipped cream. Mulligan's is available for all celebrations, meetings and receptions. Open for lunch and dinner year round. What better place to meet your friends for a drink than the new large second floor deck at Mulligan's!

Hot Shrimp, Crab & Parmesan Dip

8 oz. Cream Cheese	2 tsp. Worcestershire
8 oz. Heavy Cream	1 tsp Cayenne pepper
½ cup of grated Parmesan Cheese	2 tsp dried parsley
1 tsp prepared Horseradish	1 cup diced steamed shrimp

1 lb. Crabmeat drained (choose your own crabmeat, however we use a mixture of claw for its taste and lump for its texture). Mix all of your ingredients, top with a sprinkling of parmesan cheese and crab. Bake at 350 degrees until it bubbles around the sides and the parmesan cheese on top is browned (about 20 minutes) Serve with warm pita points, fresh tortilla chips or your choice of crackers.

North Banks

Restaurant & Raw Bar

TimBuck II Shopping Village
Corolla, North Carolina

Cindy Stevens, Owner   (252) 453-3344

North Banks can be defined as a restaurant that is casual, upscale and definitely has a touch of class thrown in. Cindy Stevens, owner, goes to work each day with the attitude that she is hosting her own party and everyone is a special guest. After meeting Cindy, I discovered an extremely hard working lady with a lot of ambition and determination. So, no wonder this restaurant is a favorite place to dine and meet new friends.

As you enter this 60 seat establishment, one of the first things you'll notice is the 28 foot vaulted ceilings, the large fish mounted on the walls, fresh stems of flowers on each table, the bar with four satellite TV's and jazz playing in the background. There's also a cozy room up front for 8 to 10 people for private dining.

North Banks features fresh locally caught tuna, mahi-mahi and flounder from Etheridge Seafood in Wanchese. They even have their own lobster tank, therefore a fresh lobster is guaranteed. The Raw Bar menu offers a selection of oysters, Maine mussels, littleneck clams, spiced shrimp, snowcrab legs and Maine lobsters. The creamy New England style Clam Chowder with a hint of sherry is a local favorite and perfect for starters.

The menu features large salads with choice of toppings, hand made half pound burgers, great selection of sandwiches, ribs, chicken and jambalaya. For lunch, try the game fish burrito or my favorite "shrimp cake sandwich" served with lemon dill sauce, lettuce and tomato. The fried seafood combination with fresh giant scallops, shrimp, select oysters and tilapia served with French fries and cole slaw is a big hit for lunch.

For dinner, choose the 8-ounce Filet Mignon, hand cut, grilled and topped with chimmichurri butter or Béarnaise. Another favorite is the "Colossal lump crab grenades" served with Asian slaw. Be sure and ask your server for the lunch or dinner specials of the day. There's so much to choose from here. Desserts are made fresh daily and selection changes often. My favorite is the authentic *Key West lime pie*, but *I love the chocolate chip pecan pie* also. *Let's face it; every dessert is my favorite,*

A children's menu is available. Full ABC permits with a carefully selected wine list. Open mid February thru Thanksgiving and Christmas for lunch and dinner.

Shrimp Cakes

1 lb. peeled shrimp	¼ tsp. salt
2 T. lemon juice	1/8 tsp. cayenne
2 T. capers	1 egg
4 T green onions	½ cup mashed potatoes
2 T. parsley	½ cup bread crumbs

Steam or boil the shrimp and chop into desired size pieces, (not to big)
Peale potatoes, Boil to stage for mashing, then drain the potatoes,
In food processor combine lemon juice, capers, green onion, parsley, salt, cayenne and egg. Pulse until blended.
Add chopped shrimp to the mixture and hand mix thoroughly. Mash cooled potatoes, (no big chunks) add to shrimp cake mixture. Mix in breadcrumbs slowly, (just enough to hold cakes together.)
Cakes should be portioned to about 5 ounces each. Mixture makes approximately 7 cakes.

Lemon Dill Sauce

1 cup grated parmesan cheese	¼ cup minced garlic
¼ cup white pepper	1 ½ T. dried basil
1 gallon mayonnaise	½ cup dried dill
1 cup apple cider vinegar	1 ½ T. dried thyme
5 lbs. sour cream	1 ½ cup lemon juice
½ cup Worcestershire sauce	4 chopped yellow onions

Process onions and cheese in food processor. Add remaining ingredients and hand mix well.

Makes 6 quarts

Ocean Boulevard
Bistro & Martini Bar

N.C Hwy. 12 (Beach Road) MP 2
Kitty Hawk, North Carolina

www.obbistro.com (252) 261-2546

Donnie King, Owner, Executive Chef Heather King, Owner
Michael Thomas, Chef-de-Cuisine Angel Doebler, PastryChef
Timothy Gard, Sous Chef

This one-of-a-kind upscale award winning restaurant is the results of Donnie Just and Donny King's thirteen successful years serving up quality cuisine at the well-known award winning 1587 Restaurant located in the Tranquil House Inn in Manteo. In 2001, King purchased Ocean Boulevard Bistro & Martini Bar and once again brought with him all the flair associated with great food and outstanding creativity.

The restaurant occupies the original Virginia Dare Hardware Store, and is now a haven for creative cocktails and sophisticated cuisine. The Martini Bar is made of simple concrete weighing four tons and other areas of dining area have exposed brick walls as well as retro glass block. The kitchen is exposed and even offers a "chefs counter" where guest can watch the culinary team in action.

This popular local restaurant features seasonal cuisine prepared by executive chef Donny King and Chef Thomas. The menu is the result of an evolving style refined over the years at "1587" by King. Selections are all prepared using locally grown herbs, spices, produce and fresh seafood. Menu changes according to season. Known for its world-class cuisine, Ocean Boulevard diners will long remember an unforgettable dining experience at this favorite spot. Ocean Boulevard has received The Wine Spectator award of Excellence from 2009 thru 2011. They also received the People's Choice award for the March of Dimes for most competitive 2011 Dish of the Outer Banks. In 2011, Chef Gard placed 2nd in the OBX Chowder Cookoff. Ocean Boulevard has been featured in the Washington Post and many other magazines.

To complement your dining experience, an extensive and impressive wine list is available along with a list of the best Martini selection found on the beach. A favorite is the "Dirty Boulevard" Martini and the "South Beach." The restaurant offers full catering service with custom menus featuring fine cuisine presented with flair on or off-premises. Reservations are suggested in season. Be sure and checkout the late Friday night bands starting around 10:30 pm and continuing to around 1:30 am. Late night plates are offered starting at 11pm.

Oyster-Saffron Stew with Smoked Bacon and Parmesan
(Makes 5 to 6 cups)

2 pints oysters'	2 oz. vegetable oil
6 strips bacon	3 cloves garlic, minced
½ cup shredded parmesan	1 pinch cayenne
12 sprigs parsley	2 pinches saffron
1 medium yellow onion	1½ cup white wine
2 medium carrots	5 cups shellfish stock or
2 ribs celery	clam juice
½ cup crimini mushrooms	2 oz. butter
(all vegetables are a medium dice)	2 oz. flour
2 ears corn, shucked and corn	1 cup heavy cream
shaved off cob	

Pick through the oysters to make sure there are no shells. Bake bacon in a 375 degree oven for about twelve minutes or till almost crispy. Let the bacon cool on paper towels and slice. Pick the leaves from the parsley sprigs and chop till very small.

Cut the vegetables in a medium dice.

In a 3 quart sauce pan (or bigger) on high heat, sweat the vegetables (except the corn and mushrooms) till the onions are translucent. Add the garlic and saffron and stir for a minute or two. Add the corn, mushrooms and cayenne and stir for another couple of minutes. Add the white wine and let boil down for five minutes. Then add the shellfish stock (if you are not able to make a shellfish stock canned ocean clam juice will do) and bring to a boil. While waiting for the soup to boil, melt the butter in a small sauté pan and mix in the flour until smooth and very warm, thus creating a roux. When the soup is boiling, whisk in the roux until well incorporated. Bring back to a boil and let simmer for two minutes. Add the heavy cream.

Pour the oysters into a large hot sauté pan. The oysters should release a little liquid. When the oysters are still pretty rare, strain the liquor off into the sink. Finish cooking the oysters (and let them release more liquid for the stew) until desired doneness. Stir into the stew and you're ready to serve.

Ladle a cup of oyster soup into six bowls and sprinkle with the cooked bacon and parmesan and serve.

Orange Blossom Café and Bakery

47208 Hwy. 12
Buxton, North Carolina

Charley Pereira, Owner   (252) 995-4109

The Orange Blossom is a great place for islanders to come together and for tourists to gather, located in the heart of "downtown" Buxton, and in eye sight of the Cape Hatteras Lighthouse. It's a great place to start your day with an array of fresh-baked sweets and just baked donuts, fluffy biscuits and fresh bagels and of course those famous Apple Uglies that you have to see to believe. There's even a chocolate covered ugly along with cinnamon rolls, cheese Danish and a whole assortment of muffins including Cranberry-Orange Blossom Muffins. Breakfast is their specialty serving eggs, breakfast burritos made with homemade salsa, bagels, and so much more. If you have a huge appetite, then try "The Buxton" made with 3 sausage patties, 6 pieces of bacon, 3 eggs, tomato and mayo served on their own homemade bread. Lee Anderson makes the biscuits and claims that his are the best in the world.

Orange Blossom Café & Bakery is considered an institution on Hatteras Island as it was originally built as the Orange Blossom Motel in the 1950's by the Barnettes and named for the orange trees that grew on the premises. After their deaths, the motel was converted to a bakery and later to a café and bakery. The restaurant is open from 6:30 a.m. until 11:00 a.m. daily serving breakfast.

Cranberry-Orange Blossom Muffins

1½ sticks butter, softened
1 1/3 c. sugar
4 large eggs
4 c. flour
4 tsp. baking powder
1 tsp. salt

2 tsp. grated orange rind
1 1/3 c. milk
½ tsp. orange extract
2 c. fresh cranberries
2/3 c. chopped pecans

In an electric mixer, cream the butter and sugar. Beat in the eggs one at a time. Combine the flour, baking powder, salt and orange rind. Beat the flour mixture and milk alternately into the creamed mixture. Add the orange extract and fold into the cranberries and pecans. Scoop into 12 well greased muffin cups and bake in a 350-degree oven until an inserted toothpick comes out clean. Cool on a wire rack for a few minutes and remove muffins from pan. Spread tops with orange icing.

Orange Icing

1 ¾ c. powdered sugar   2 T. orange marmalade
2 T. orange juice

Heat the marmalade briefly to liquefy. Place sugar in the bowl of an electric mixer and beat in the orange juice and marmalade to obtain a spreading consistency.

Ortega'z

Southwestern Grill and Wine Bar

201 Sir Walter Raleigh Street
Manteo, North Carolina

www.ortegaz.com   (252) 473-5911

Lisa and Marcello Ortega, Owners

When the Green Dolphin Pub decided to close this location after so many years, local residents weren't sure what would happen to the building. Lisa and Marcello Ortega were looking for a place to open up their own restaurant and use their thirty-two years of combined restaurant experience and the Pub was just that place. The Ortega's took all of the previous restaurant best attributes and used them in renovating the building along with a lot of personal touches to make it one of the most popular neighborhood restaurants in the area.

During the renovation of the building in 2007, the Ortega's discovered remnants of past businesses. The walls of an old ESSO gas station were slowly revealed dating back to the early 1930's and 1940's when Milton Midgett and Maywood Lee had run the station. A section of the gas station wall can still be seen today. Remnants of a past fire and flood water lines also came to light. On another wall of the restaurant is the original mural painting of the Albatross fishing fleet of Hatteras that still is in operation today.   The Pub was such a landmark in Manteo that an episode of Matlock, the Andy Griffith television drama was filmed there.

Marcel learned at an early age the art of cooking from his mother, the old fashioned way, in the kitchen. Therefore, everything they serve is made fresh and from scratch. The chips and salsa are hand cut and made daily. The house roasted beef, chicken and pork are slow roasted and hand pulled. Lunch includes soups, salads, sandwiches, wraps and more. For starters try their house made stuffed jalapeno poppers dipped into a dark beer batter then fried and topped with pineapple salsa. Another favorite is the Ortega'z chop house salad. All salads are available with chicken, steak, and shrimp as an extra.   Another lunch favorite is Linda's famous crab & wild mushroom cheesecake made with jumbo lump crabmeat.

This restaurant should definitely be on your list to visit while on the Outer Banks. There's a great selecton of dinner entrees such as Ortega'z B.Y.O.B.— build your own brochette (kabob) served on a bed of baked rice, skewer of vegetable and your choice of steak, shrimp, chicken, scallops, chorizo , vegetable or any combination. The marinated lamb shank is also a favorite along with the pork spareribs.   Steaks, crab cakes, scallops, seafood trio, grilled shrimp are all winners. The presentation of each plate is impressive and you won't go away hungry. Prices are very affordable.

As you enter the main dining room, strait ahead is a large stainless steel wine bar with mirrored walls and tall bar tables for that intimate meeting. This is a great place to gather with friends or to meet new ones. On warm sunny days, be sure to dine on the patio.

Take out and call-ahead orders are available and <u>unlimited catering service</u>. This is a kid friendly restaurant. Ortega'z is open daily except Sundays. Call for winter hours. Reservations accepted year round. Full ABC license.

Ortega'z Fire Roasted Corn Chowder

3   slices of Applewood smoked bacon-chopped
1   large yellow onion-chopped
4   ribs of celery-chopped
1   tbsp. fresh ground black pepper
1   tbsp. kosher salt
2   tbsp. thyme leaves
¼ cup cilantro-chopped
1   qt. flour
1   lb. butter
1   cup chicken stock
10 qts. Half and half
1 ½ gal. Yukon gold potatoes-1/4 inch cubes
3   quarts yellow corn kernels

Procedure:
1. Boil Potatoes until tender-drain and reserve
2. Lay corn out on baking sheet, drizzle with olive oil and dust with salt and pepper. Roast in oven at 350 degrees until lightly browned
3. In large pot, sauté chopped bacon until cooked through approximately 5 minutes
4. Add butter, and bring to a slow simmer
5. Add onion and celery, cook until onions are translucent
6. Add pepper, salt, cilantro, thyme leaves, and cook for 5 minutes
7. Add flour and cook an additional 10 minutes. Stirring constantly
8. Add water and chicken stock, cook until soup thickens approximately 10-12 minutes
9. Add potatoes and roasted corn
10. Slowly add half and half
11. Cook under low heat until soup thickens
Serve with garnish of fresh avocado slice, and toasted pita points.

Owens Restaurant

Mile post 16 1/2, Beach Road
Nags Head, North Carolina

Owens Family, Owners   (252) 441-7309
Clara Mae Shannon, Operator

Is Owens Restaurant a great restaurant or an institution on the Outer Banks? Of course, the answer has to be, both. Owens Restaurant was established in 1946 by Bob and Clara Owens. Their goal was to serve only the freshest seafood and shellfish at a reasonable price, and make the customer feel like family. Owens is still run that way after 55 years. Over the years the family has collected many nautical artifacts that are displayed in the restaurant. Remnants of letters from long ago from those who manned the old Coast Guard stations still wait to be read. No visit to the Outer Banks would be complete without a visit to this historic restaurant. Bob and Clara would be proud to know that their children, grandchildren, and great-grandchildren are still carrying on their proud tradition.

Owens now focuses more on classic Southern coastal cuisine, such as shrimp and grits, or pecan-encrusted Carolina catfish. Miss O' crabcakes and pastas are among the most popular entrees. The menu features fresh Maine lobster, aged Angus beef, ribs, pasta, fresh produce and herbs. The homemade desserts are definitely worth saving room for. Open for dinner in season. Call for winter hours.

Owen's Hush Puppies

2 ½ c. self-rising flour   1 tsp. salt
1.c. white cornmeal   1 egg
2/3 c. sugar   1 ¼ c. cold water
1 T. baking powder   ¼ c. evaporated milk

Mix first 5 ingredients thoroughly; add egg and blend in well. Combine milk with cold water; pour all liquid into the dry mixture. Mix gently but quickly, just enough to blend everything together. Allow to rest 10 minutes at room temperature; drop by rounded teaspoonfuls into 325-degree vegetable oil. Fry, rolling frequently, until golden brown; 6 to 8 minutes. Dip spoon in cold water after dropping each spoonful.

Pamlico Jack's
Pirate Hideaway
U.S. Hwy. 158 Bypass, MP 16
Nags Head, North Carolina   (252) 441-2637

Mike Kelly, Owner   Tom Sloate, General Manager
Lee Miller, Executive Chef   Steve Scott, Pastry Chef

Located on the beautiful Roanoke Sound, this former Penguin Isle restaurant has just undergone an extensive remodel with a much more casual atmosphere as a family and adult-edge pirate theme restaurant that's fun for all. Chef Lee and his original staff will now be creating island inspired cuisine straight from the galley along with your favorites you've come to enjoy over the years at Penguin Isle. Pamlico Jack's will carry on the legacy of being the winner of The Wine Spectator's Award of Excellence for its wine list as "one of the best in the world" for the past twenty years. The Food Network awarded it "The Best of Waterfront Dining." They were also awarded the "People Choice Award" Taste of the Beach 2007 and the "Crab Cake cook-off", best of the beach 2008.

Fresh local seafood, chicken, handmade pasta, Black Angus beef and fresh-baked breads are only a part of their offerings. All the desserts are delectable. Enjoy the new Rum Jumpers deck bar overlooking the sound where spectacular sunsets can be enjoyed while having an Island cocktail before dinner. Call for entertainment schedule aboard the pirate ship outdoor bar. Little Pirates menu available.

Bayou Sea Scallops on Angel Hair Pasta
Serves 4

2 TBSP Olive Oil
2 8 oz. Scallops, remove foot (medium size 1- 1oz per scallop)
3 TBSP Bayou Spice
2 tomatoes, roughly chopped, seedless, skinless
½ cup scallions, chopped
3 TBSP butter
½ cup beer (the chef's favorite is BUD)
1 serving of cooked Angel Hair Pasta

Heat olive oil to medium heat. Toss scallops in Bayou Spice. Sauté scallops until half done, slight color, 1-2 minutes. Add tomatoes, scallions/toss for 20 seconds. Add beer, butter/let foam and reduce until scallops are cooked to a hot medium rare. Pour over cooked pasta and serve.

Bayou Spice:

½ TBSP Salt	2 TBSP Annulated Garlic	2 TBSP Annulated Onion
2 TBSP Thyme	2 TBSP Basil	2 TBSP Cayenne Pepper
2 TBSP Paprika	¾ TSP Rosemary	

Peppercorn's Restaurant & Lounge

Ramada Plaza
1701 Virginia Dare Trail MP 9.5
Kill Devil Hills, North Carolina

Sterling Webster, General Manager   Greg Sniegowski, Executive Chef
Lou Hunt, Sous Chef   Wanda Daniels, Sous Chef

(252) 441-2151 Ext. 665

Ocean views are spectacular at this great restaurant overlooking the Atlantic. You can dine and watch the pelicans glide over the waves or the moon rise over the ocean while enjoying a delightful dinner. Their classically trained chefs bring a combination of Regional dishes, Multi-ethnic foods as well as a very creative cosmopolitan flair to the menu.

Local favorites include Atlantic salmon stuffed with crabmeat, and prime rib crusted with spices and served au jus. Crabcakes are also a favorite, seasoned with just the right amount of spices. A Surf and Turf special is served every Wednesday and Saturday year –round. Each entrée is served with "potato of the day" or wild rice blend and fresh vegetables and a basket of breads. You'll definitely want to try some of the wonderful desserts. For lunch, you'll want to try the giant Portabello mushroom stuffed with spiced crabmeat and melted cheese or the soups, salads, and sandwiches.

An outside Gazebo deck bar offers lunch with live acoustic music from 1-6 p.m. daily in season. There's a full bar with live entertainment nightly during the summer. Peppercorns provides take-out food and room service for Ramada guests. A children's menu is available. Open for breakfast, lunch, and dinner year round. Treat yourself to an early breakfast and watch the sun rise over the ocean. You'll be glad you did.

Peppercorns Signature Stuffed Oysters

Ingredients:
Fresh raw oysters on the half shell

Stuffing Mixture:
Andouille Sausage, diced in small cubes
Gouda cheese, diced in small cubes
Mix ingredients together and top the raw oysters with a generous
amount of the stuffing mixture. Broil in oven until browned. Serve
with lemon wedge for garnish.

Portobello Mushroom Stuffed With Crabmeat

2 tablespoon Olive oil
1 teaspoon crushed garlic
4 ounces fresh lump crabmeat
2 ounces shredded Cheddar, Swiss or Parmesan cheese
Juice of 1 lemon
Dash of Old Bay seasoning, salt and pepper

Method:
1. Preheat oven to broil.
2. 1 large Portobello mushroom cap, stem removed
   Marinate mushroom cap in olive oil and crushed garlic for 15 min.
3. Top mushroom with remaining ingredients, sprinkling the shredded
   cheese on top.
4. Place on a lightly oiled baking pan.
5. Put under preheated broiler until heated through and cheese is
   melted and light brown. Approximately 5 to 7 minutes.
6. Serve whole with a salad and dressing of choice or cut into wedges
   and serve as an appetizer.

   Serves 1 as Entrée or 2 as an Appetizer

Pier House Restaurant

(Located on the Nags Head Fishing Pier)
3335 South Virginia Dare Trail, M.P. 11.5
Nags Head, North Carolina

Captain Andy and Louie McCann, Owner   (252) 441-5141 or 441-4200
Louie McCann, Julie Ann White, cooks   Jim Williams, Night Chef

Good things in life come and go, but thank goodness for the Nags Head Fishing Pier and restaurant that has challenged hurricanes and "nor'easters" since 1947. It's definitely seen its days of destruction losing sections of pier, even being totally destroyed during the Ash Wednesday storm of 1962 only to be rebuilt again to battle more Atlantic storms. The popularity among tourists and locals make this seafood restaurant a must do. The views, cozy atmosphere, and the sound of the ocean roaring beneath you while dining is why we love this restaurant, there's no other place like it on the Outer Banks. The Pier House restaurant was established in 1980 with Joe Justis as owner. In 1985 Captain Andy and Louie purchased the Nags Head Pier and restaurant. Louie runs the restaurant and Andy runs the pier now.

This is the only restaurant that I know of on the Outer Banks that advertises. "You Hook 'Em ~ We Cook "Em" as long as you clean the catch. They're serve your catch (up to 10oz) the way you like "em" with fries, slaw and hush puppies. Breakfast is a big here with the fishing crowd starting at 7a.m. with favorites that you won't find on menus elsewhere such as the fried salt herring, fried sea trout and herring roe. But there's the old favorites, omlettes, hot cakes, creamed chip beef and country ham, bacon. Bloodymary, screwdriver and greyhound beverages are available along with the regulars.

Menu items include appetizers, steamer items, soups, salads, seafood and specialty sandwiches. Start off your meal with a cup of Pier Pressure Chowder filled with chunks of tuna, shrimp, clams and scallops in a rich broth or a salad topped with your favorite seafood. Choose from fried seafood baskets, 18 selections of sandwiches, chef specials including flamed grilled steak, softshelled crabs, and catch of the day, seafood platters, and chicken. The food is excellent. Full ABC license. You won't leave this restaurant hungry, that's for sure. Little fishermen menu available. Open spring though late fall for breakfast, lunch, dinner.

Grilled Steak Salad

Ingredients:
1 Flank steak   6 to 8 pitted Kalamata olives
Salt/Pepper to taste   Roasted red pepper
1 head Romaine   Crumbled Blue cheese
1 vine ripe tomato, halved

Season flank steak with salt and pepper and grill to desired temperature. Clean Romaine lettuce and chop, place on serving plate. Cut your tomato in wedge pieces and place around the rim of the salad, place your olives in the lettuce, slice your roasted red pepper and place on lettuce bed, sprinkle Blue cheese crumbles all over. Slice 4 -5 pieces of your flank steak on the bias and top off the salad. Serve with a dressing of choice. I recommend a balsamic vinaigrette.

Poor Richards Sandwich Shop

303 Queen Elizabeth Ave.
Manteo, North Carolina

Ted Clissold, Owner   (252) 473-3333

The setting is the historical Manteo waterfront on Roanoke Island with the sailing ship "Elizabeth II" anchored in the background. This cozy sandwich shop occupies a well know landmark site for the community. The original building was owned by Mr. Jolliff and used as a machine shop and the first "Western Union location". In 1939 a fire destroyed the original structure and later was replaced by the present day building. The sandwich shop opened in 1984 in the back section of the building with a local radio station occupying the front part of the building. The original old pine floors and brick walls remain but the radio station has been replaced with Poor Richards Pub where locals and tourist gather.

Poor Richards is your neighborhood destination for breakfast or lunch. Prices here are very reasonable. It's a casual place where you order at the counter, pick a seat and they'll bring your order to the table. Seating is available inside or outside on the patio overlooking Shallowbag Bay. For breakfast, waffles, eggs, omlettes, breakfast burritos, grits, pancakes, sausage and bacon are served. The lunch menu features deli sandwiches, burgers, hot dogs, BBQ, phillys, fries, salads, wraps. This sandwich shop is known for its grilled Reuben sandwich, turkey salad and chili. Don't forget the daily specials

Beer and wine are available. Open year round for breakfast and lunch. Poor Richards Pub is open year round with live music on Thursday, Friday and Saturday nights. Check for entertainment schedule.

Chili
(Makes 10 gallons)

6 qt. large chopped onions	2 cups cumin
16 oz. minced garlic	2/3 cup salt
6 lbs. chopped green peppers	1/3 cup black pepper
2 cups olive oil	1 cup Worcestershire
2 large #10 cans diced tomatoes	1 cup Texas Pete
2 large cans #10 crushed tomatoes	2 lbs. TVP (textured vegetable
3 cups chili powder	protein)
	4 large #10 cans beans

Sauté onions, garlic, green peppers and olive oil together. In large pot combine other ingredients. Cook on low, stirring frequently to keep from scorching. Note: The TVP is a vegetable protein that responds differently as to how much liquid is needed; therefore do not add all the TVP at once. You might need to add more water to mixture.

Port O' Call Restaurant

Virginia Dare Road (Beach Road) MP 8 ½
Kill Devil Hills, N.C. 27948

Frank H. Gajar, Owner   (252) 441-7484
Adam Lindstrom, Chef

The Port O' Call was founded in 1965 and has been in continuous operation ever since. In 1983, a major renovation and expansion was undertaken to add a gift shop and lounge. In 2004, the gift emporium was expanded again. This restaurant is beach casual with family dining in mind.

The lounge features live entertainment and dancing every night, in season, and the gift shop is open year-round. The interior design of the Port O' Call is turn of the century Victorian with period furniture and collectibles throughout.

The menu features a large selection of fresh seafood...steamers, steaks, prime rib, pasta, ribs, and chicken, including a children's menu. A Buffet is served on all major holidays. Enjoy early bird specials from 4:30-6:30 p.m.

Caribbean Jerk Tuna

2 lbs. Tuna Filets
1 tbsp. Caribbean Jerk Seasoning
¼ cup white wine
¼ cup orange juice
1 tsp. White pepper
¼ cup fresh cilantro
Combine seasoning, pepper, cilantro and liquids. Pour over filets and bake in 350 degrees oven for 10 minutes.

Meanwhile, heat together the following:
1 8 oz. can coconut milk
1 tsp. brown sugar
1 tsp. crab base
Heat until sugar and crab base are dissolved.

To this mixture add:
¼ cup chopped green onion
¼ cup each, diced yellow, green and sweet red peppers
½ cup fresh pineapple chunks
Cook over medium to low heat for 15 minutes. Add 1/8 tsp. crushed red pepper and ¼ cup lemon juice. Heat for 2-3 minutes. Add salt to taste. Pour over filets and garnish with toasted coconut.

Red Sky Café

1197 Duck Road
Duck, North Carolina

Wes and Cindy Stepp, Owners
Wes Stepp, Chef

(252) 261-8646
www.redskycafe.com

This restaurant located right in the heart of Duck opened in 2002 and has quickly become a favorite with Wes Stepp as its new owner and chef. Wes is no stranger to the Outer Banks as he was the former executive chef at Kelly's restaurant for many years. Eating is an adventure at this eclectic but casual restaurant. Chef Wes does his magic with a seasonally changing menu of inventive combination of Coastal cuisine and "Southern cuisine with surprising international nuances".

On a recent visit, I was seated next to a young couple from New Jersey that were so enthused about the restaurant and the food that they decided to dine there for the third time that week before returning home. Well, I call that true dedication.

If you love fresh baked breads of all different types, then the racks of bread stacked high will definitely catch your attention. All are available for purchase and are baked daily on premises. Northern breads such as biallys hard rolls, foccacia and cinnamon rolls are favorites.

Red Sky Café's lunch menu includes delicious sandwiches, wraps, soups, wood fired pizzas, quesadilla, wood fired baby back ribs, pastas, cheeseburgers, salads and so much more. Wes' menu is always supplemented by at least a half dozen daily specials. Look for Wes' soup of the day. Dinners are excellent, especially the pesto seared tuna steak, or the shrimp & scallops, coconut fried jumbo shrimp and the crab cakes. Chef Wes pairs a large selection of wine with its many flavors. The desserts are made fresh daily by Cindy Stepp and are as pleasing to the palate as they are to the eye.

Red Sky Café also offers full creative meals "Gourmet to Go". Create with Wes the meal for your group, "large or small". A variety of wine is also available to select from by the bottle or glass along with a martini menu and a variety of mixed drinks.

There's a good selection of items available for those little southern bells and little gents. Open year round, call for winter hours.

French Market Flounder
(Served with Cilantro Lime Slaw and Blackeyed and Chick Pea Rice Salad)

Flounder filets	Fresh basil
Plain Flour	Summer tomato
Eggs	Romano or Asiago cheese
White wine	Salt & Pepper
Lemon	

Dip flounder filets into beaten eggs and then into flour. Sprinkle with salt and pepper to taste. Pan sauté flounder with flesh side down in skillet with just enough olive oil for browning on both sides. Next, sprinkle Romano or Asiago cheese and basil over top of flounder. Add one tomato slice over top of each. Place flounder with cheese, tomatoes in oven for a few minutes on 400 degrees. Do not over cook.

Cilantro Lime Slaw

Small head of cabbage – shredded
Cilantro ½ cup – diced and fresh
½ cup olive oil
¼ cup rice wine vinegar
¼ cup honey
Salt and pepper
Combine and let chill for 30 minutes. Finish with juice of 2 limes.

Rice Salad

3 cups cooked white rice
½ cup black-eyed peas
   (cooked tender or rinsed from can)
½ cup chickpeas (rinsed from can)
Small red onion – diced
¼ cup each yellow and red pepper,
   diced

¼ cup olive oil
¼ cup rice wine vinegar
2 tablespoons of basil
   (cut in strips)
Salt and pepper
Pinch of sugar

Combine all ingredients and serve.

Roadside Raw Bar & Grill
1193 Duck Road
Duck, North Carolina

Mark & Ashley Copeland, Owner   (252) 261-5729
Ben Schrader, Head Chef

The Roadside Bar and Grill is located in an antique cottage in the heart of Duck Village. The structure was originally built in 1932 by Mr. & Mrs. J.C. Hines as their residence. It was one of the first homes in Duck. The building has also been used as a real estate office and a retail shop. The renovations, which created the restaurant, began in November of 1994. The floors were stripped down to their original hard wood, an open-air kitchen was created, and a large brick patio was added. The doors opened for business in May 1995.

Set back and enjoy live Jazz on the patio every Tuesday and Thursday night in season. The Roadside is just a great place to relax and get in tune with the quaint surroundings of Duck.

The following recipe is a good representation of the menu at The Roadside. Chef Schrader uses only the freshest ingredients. He buys the fish from local fishermen and the produce from a Wanchese farm, and then adds a great deal of imagination and creativity during the preparation. Seafood, Steaks, Lobster and fantastic salads are just a sample of what's on their menu. I just happen to be crazy about their" Roadside Salad" made with Mesclun greens, fresh fruits, raisins and toasted pistachios with raspberry vinaigrette. The desserts are wonderful, but my favorite is the chocolate bread pudding with rich caramel and chocolate sauce.

Open for lunch and dinner daily. Call for winter hours.

Bronzed Tuna

with Portabello-Ardsville Sesame Orzo & Mango Salsa

Bronzed Tuna:

10 oz. tuna steak
1 tsp. cayenne
1 tsp. red pepper
1 tsp. crushed red pepper
1 tsp. black pepper
1 tsp. salt

1 tsp. oregano
1 tsp. rosemary
1 tsp. thyme
3½ T. sugar
¾ c. oil

Orzo:

2 c. cooked orzo
3 T. diced Andsville sausage
3 T. diced roasted portabello
4 T. sesame oil

1 T. kosher salt
1 tsp. white pepper
1 T. Caribbean jerk

Mango Salsa:

1 c. mango diced
3 T. diced red onion
3 T. diced red pepper
3 T. diced scallions

2 squeezed limes
1 tsp. cayenne
2 oz. Malibu rum

Bronze Mix: Add all ingredients together until they form a smooth paste.

Orzo: Mix cooked orzo and ingredients and saute lightly.

Salsa: Add all ingredients and refrigerate.

Cooking and Serving: In well ventilated area, heat skillet on high heat. Dredge tuna in bronze mix until well coated. Sear on both sides of tuna and place on top of sauteed orzo mix, then top with mango salsa.

Route 12
Steak & Seafood Company & Raw Bar
Timbuck II Shopping Village
Corolla, North Carolina

Mark Grizzard, President, Owner   (252) 453-4644
Stephen Hilliker, Co-Owner
"Finely" Ron Davidson, Executive Chef

I'll have to say that I was impressed with this restaurant the minute I entered and was greeted by the friendly staff. Entering its seventh season, Route 12 bills itself as "the restaurant with the finest staff, pride and attention to detail and superb service that every table and guest receive when dining" It's almost as if the managers and wait staff know what, you as a guest, want before you know you want or ask for it.

Here, the decor is tropical, with displays of local and not so local art. Walls are painted a pale yellow with black accents, and window treatments of tropical palm trees swaying add a feeling of relaxation to your dining pleasure.

The food here is prepared by one of the Outer Banks most noted chefs, "Chef Ron Davidson," He's been on the Outer Banks for almost twenty years as a chef. He prepares some of the most delicious dishes you'll find anywhere. You will not go away hungry at this restaurant, proportions are large and you don't have to break the bank to dine here. There's even a child's menu.

The menu features traditional Outer Banks local seafood and choice steaks, ribs, pastas, raw bar items and even lobster tails for the little ones. Be sure and try the Portobella Napoleon appetizer, its two marinated Portobella mushrooms stacked high with sliced tomatoes, Mozzarella, eggplant, applewood smoked bacon, and topped with fresh pesto. Its definitely a favorite along with the" Baked Oysters Down East" topped with lobster and mushrooms served with a hollandaise sauce.

Entrees like Chef Ron's "Ahi Pepper Filet" yellow fin tuna wrapped with applewood smoked bacon, topped with cracked peppercorns, grilled and served over baby spinach and a green peppercorn and garlic demi glace is a favorite along with "Route 12's Famous Pork Ribs. Nightly specials are also available. The Outer Banks Seafood Platters are a good deal also, so pay close attention.

There's a full bar where wine, beer, mixed drinks are served. A carefully selected wine list with prices you won't see elsewhere is available. A child's menu is available. Open for dinner only. "To go menu" is available. Reservations recommended in season.

Rundown Café

North Virginia Dare Trail (Beach Road)   MP 1
Kitty Hawk, North Carolina

Michael Montiel, Owner   (252) 255-0026

Caribbean flavors join local seafood to create the theme of this locals' favorite dining spot. Opened in 1993, this popular restaurant was an expansion of the tropics for the northern beaches and quickly became a vacationer's favorite. The Caribbean-themed menu and the tropical island décor have kept year round residents returning to this spot.

Named for a Jamaican stew, Rundown serves favorites such as stuffed chicken with sautéed spinach and feta cheese oven roasted and toped with a roasted red pepper sauce. Other favorites include the Rundown Noodles, Caribbean style vegetarian rice noodles with sautéed veggies in a spicy Thai sauce topped with ground peanuts and lime. Exciting and ever-changing specials are listed on boards inside the restaurant. The homemade desserts are definitely worth trying, especially the dark chocolate brownie and cheesecake that changes flavors every few weeks.

The Tsunami Bar is located upstairs where you can kick back and be with the gang. A large vibrant mural covers one wall of this earth tone room and a deck is just outside of the bar area. Rundown Café is a place you'll feel comfortable, no matter what your age or lifestyle. There's a cultural, social-economic barrier-less crowd that you find here. Open daily serving lunch and dinner. Call for winter hours.

St. Martin Shrimp

1 yellow onion julienned
48 peeled and deveined shrimp (31-35) ct.
2 bulbs garlic, chopped
3 tomatoes, diced
¼ cup sundried tomatoes julienned
8 pieces of bacon, cooked and chopped
¼ cup olive oil

chopped parsley
½ stick butter
salt and pepper
½ cup white wine
1 small box of
  linguini, cooked

Get olive oil hot in large skillet. Sauté garlic & onion. Cook til garlic starts to brown, add bacon and shrimp, sauté on high til starting to turn pink, add fresh tomatoes and sundried tomatoes, toss, Add white wine and let cook 2 minutes. Add salt, pepper to taste, let reduce, then toss in whole butter and chopped parsley. Drop pasta in hot salted water, Separate in 4 bowls. Top with shrimp mixture. Serve with parmesan cheese, and a piece of crusty French bread. Enjoy!!!   Serves 4   P.S. You can't add enough garlic!

Sam & Omie's

Virginia Dare Trail (Beach Road) MP 16 1/2
Whalebone Junction
Nags Head, North Carolina

Mike Merritt, Owner   (252) 441-7366
Carole Sykes, Owner   Darlene Anderson, Breakfast cook

No trip to the Outer Banks would be complete without a visit to one of the oldest restaurants left on the beach. Not a whole lot has changed since its founding in 1937 when Sam Tillet and his son Omie opened Sam & Omie's as a fishing center. Sam started cooking breakfast for the men going out on the fishing boats in the mornings. In the late 1960s, the fishing center closed and the restaurant continued operating full time.

The restaurant exterior still has that "Old Nags Head Traditional style" that we have come to associate with, as true "Outer Banks". The gas pump that once stood out front has been replaced with a sign now but much of the original charm and character still remains. The old wooden floors are still there but have been spruced up a bit from the days of no varnish and sandy floors. The pool table that I remember many years ago has since been removed and replaced with tables. The old original fishing center countertop is now being used for the bar. If walls could talk, this restaurant would definitely have a lot to say. Sam & Omie's celebrated their 70th Anniversary in 2007.

Today, the restaurant is owned by Mike Merritt and Carole Sykes. Carole came to work for the summer as a waitress and had her life changed forever. Sam & Omie's has changed ownership several times throughout the years but when Carole and former owner, Teresa Merrrit, now deceased, heard that their former employer was selling the restaurant, they knew they had to purchase it. Carole and all the employees take pride in carrying on the traditions that have made Sam & Omie's so much a part of the Outer Banks. Darlene is still the breakfast cook and has been with the restaurant for over 31 years. Michael Clough has been with the restaurant for five years cooking the same dinner specials on Tuesday's and

Thursday's. Spaghetti is the special on Tuesday and Prime Rib is Thursday's special.

The restaurant is very casual with wooden booths and tables and a full service bar. There's a TV for viewing and you never know who might be sitting next to you. After all, local politicians, actors, football players and fisherman all love this place. Locals and visitors love this place, including me.

Breakfast is a big thing here with "Omie" lettes served with grits or hash browns and toast or biscuits or order the Hot cakes or one of the breakfast specials. Eggs Benedict is served on Saturday and Sunday. The lunch menu has a great variety of sandwiches from hamburgers to hot dogs, grilled chicken, clam dogs, barbecue, even an veggie sprout sandwich. Of course, the dinner menu has steak and plenty seafood to choose from including the "Whale" of a Seafood platter that includes fried or broiled clams, oysters scallops shrimp and fish and served with choice of two vegetables. Appetizers include shrimp, soft shell crab or fried oysters, clams, wings. Salads are also on the menu. Friday and Saturdays dinners feature seafood specials. The she-crab soup is great. Look for the blackboard for additional specials & homemade desserts. Dinner is served anytime after 12 p.m.

Prices are very reasonable. Draft, domestic and imported beers, house wines and mixed drinks are available. Sam & Omie's is open seven days a week for breakfast, lunch, dinner in season. Call for winter hours.

Sam and Omie's Fresh Wahoo Salad

3 lbs. fresh Wahoo
3 TBL. lemon Juice
6 eggs hard boiled and chopped
1 red pepper minced
1 cup minced green onion
3 TBL. Fresh lime juice
Salt
Lemon pepper, black pepper, white pepper and salt to taste
1 cup mayonnaise
1 cup plain yogurt

Cook fish in lemon juice and salted water and let cool. Add remaining ingredients, mix well and chill.

Stripers Bar & Grille

1100 South Bay Drive, Unit 1E (turn beside McDonalds)
Manteo, North Carolina

www.stripersbarandgrille.com   (252) 475-1021

Ed Groce, Owner

Alfredo Lanzuri, Chef, General Manager .   Jamie Dean, Chef

This Manteo restaurant is located on Shallowbag Bay, right in the middle of an oasis of the Shallowbag Bay Clubs Condo's. It's hard to detect from amongst the shadows of the surrounding condos, but just follow the road to the end and you're there. The Views are magnificent from all three levels of this octagon-shaped restaurant. Boater patrons will love this restaurant with guest boat slips available for dining or just stopping in for drinks. You won't have to break the bank to dine here, prices are reasonable and portions are large, half plate portions are also available. The atmosphere is casual but the interior of the restaurant has a touch of elegance added with its knotty pine trim and high vaulted ceilings on the third level.

Each floor of this restaurant is independent of each other with the first floor featuring the "Bearded Clam Raw & Steam Bar." This is definitely where all the action is if you dropping in for a drink, seafood, or taking a break while cruising the waters of the Outer Banks. The steam bar menu features half price specials daily from: 3:30- 5:30 p.m. daily. The bamboo steamer pots just happen to be the signature item on the raw bar menu with a choice of marinated chicken or rockfish fillets. Be sure and check out the blackboard for daily specials.

The main dining area is located on the second level with panoramic views of Shallowbag Bay and Jockey Ridge in the distance. The third level is for more intimate dining with cavernous ceilings, wind-sail fans and a cupola.

The menu specializes in items such as local seafood, steaks, sandwiches, soups, pastas. Everything is made in-house. The Stripers Rockfish is definitely worth trying; it's topped with chipotle soy mustard and wasabi aolii and served with fiesta rice and seasonable vegetables, or try the pan seared crusted crab cakes. The appetizers list feature a great crab dip, but make sure you try the "Blackened Scallops" or Tuna Sashimi . I love the Lobster bisque, Striper's own original recipe. Sandwiches, Cobb and Caesar salads are also featured. A favorite entrée is the stuffed flounder filled with back fin crab meat and topped with lemon caper cream sauce. Small plates are also available. Don't forget to try the desserts, they're great.

Open for lunch and dinner year round and serving Sunday brunch. Full ABC license on all three floors. . Children welcome, kids menu available.

Pork BBQ

4# pork Butt	2 cups cider vinegar
1# Spanish onion, sliced thin	2 tbs. coarse ground black pepper
2 tbs. crushed red pepper flakes	2 tbs. salt

1. Cut pork so it lays flat in a deep baking pan with the fat side up. This will allow the pork to cook evenly.
2. Pour the vinegar over the pork and add the remaining ingredients over the pork butt.
3. Cover with aluminum foil. Bake in a 300-degree oven for 3 ½ hours or until fork tender.
4. Remove from the oven and remove the foil.
5. Let cool to room temp in its juice. Strain off the juice (reserve the juice for other use), leaving enough juice to keep the meat moist.
6. Remove any excess fat and discard. Pull the pork and mix well.
7. If the pork is dry, add some of the reserved juice.

Yield: 6   6 oz. portions

Chipotle BBQ Sauce

1-28oz. can crushed tomatoes	1 ½ oz. Bourbon
¼ cup tomato paste	14 oz. ketchup
¼ cup W-sauce	½ cup peach daiquiri mix
½ cup apple cider vinegar	2 tsp. salt
½ cup water	2 tsp. coarse grind black pepper
½ cup brown sugar, dark	2 tsp. Chipotle, canned, purred

1. Place all ingredients in a heavy bottom pot.
2. Bring to a boil, stirring often to prevent scorching.
3. Reduce heat to a simmer and cook for 45 minutes.
4. When done, let sit in pot for 1 hour before transferring to storage container. *Yield: 1 Quart*

Hot Vinegar

12 oz. Apple cider vinegar
6 oz. dark brown sugar
1 tsp. J.O. spice
1 tsp. crushed hot red pepper flakes

1. Place all ingredients in a heavy bottom sauce pot.
2. Bring to a boil and simmer for 5 minutes.
3. Turn off heat and let sit in pot for 15 minutes before transferring to a storage container. *Yields: 2 cups*

Sugar Creek

Nags Head Manteo Causeway
Nags Head, North Carolina

Ervin Bateman, Owner

(252) 441-4963

Sugar Creek has been a favorite dining restaurant spot of visitors and locals alike since 1981. Formerly know as RV's, the restaurant has recently received a facelift with a new addition added with more seating. Located on the beautiful Roanoke Sound and Sugar Creek, dining here is to enjoy the best views and sunsets that the Outer Banks has to offer. Before dining, don't miss the opportunity to take a stroll along the dock.

There's no better place to enjoy true Carolina seafood in a casual and laid back atmosphere other than Sugar Creek. They are known for their generous portions, great prices and treating guest as family. The Seafood Stew (recipe below) is a favorite amongst guest. Only the freshest seafood is served here, along with steak, prime rib, pasta, chicken, ribs, salads, sandwiches, soups, appetizers and burgers. Appetizers, steamed seafood, drink specials are served at the gazebo raw bar from June—Labor Day. There's also a full service bar inside.

Sugar Creek is open from mid February through November serving lunch and dinner seven days a week. A children's menu is provided.

Seafood Stew

1 slice bacon, chopped	1 tsp. salt
3 stalks celery, coarsely chopped	½ tsp. pepper
1 carrot, peeled and shredded	1 tsp. Old Bay seasoning
½ onion, diced	½ tsp. lemon pepper seasoning

Simmer above ingredients, stirring frequently until celery is about three-fourths cooked. Add ½ gal. Shrimp stock—either made from shrimp base or boiled shrimp shells. Add 3 lb. fresh diced tomatoes (3 lb. can of salsa style diced tomatoes may be substituted). Bring to boil.

Add 2 lbs. raw (70/90 count), peeled and deveined shrimp along with 1 lb. scallops. Sea scallops are preferred but Bay scallops may be substituted. Return to a boil to be sure seafood is completely cooked.

Reduce heat to low. Add 1-1/2 lb. of raw, diced potatoes, (diced baby red potatoes may be substituted). Cover and allow potatoes to cook on low heat for about ½ hour, stirring occasionally.

Makes approximately 1 ½ -2 gallons

Tale of the Whale Restaurant

7575 S. Virginia Dare Trail
Nags Head/Manteo Causeway
Nags Head, North Carolina

Dan & Kathy Bibey, Owners   (252) 441-7332
Carole Bibey, Owner   taleofthewhalenagshead.com

For spectacular views of the Roanoke Sound and the small islands beyond and some of the finest seafood around, you'll be hard pressed to find any better than The Tale of the Whale Restaurant. Every seat in the dining areas offers an outstanding view of the sound. Diners nightly can see the lights of the Bodie Island Lighthouse in the distance.

Only the finest and freshest seafood, prime rib, pastas, and choice steaks and specialties of the house are served. The menu is comprehensive with an additional full menu of entrees with smaller portions just right for those of you on that special diet. You won't go away hungry after eating here.

The restaurant opened its doors in 1980 with Don & Carole Bibey as owners. They chose the name, "Tale of the Whale" because no one else at the time was using the whale motif and since Don & Carole were both interested in "saving the whales" the name was chosen. After the passing of Don in 1997, Carole continued the tradition of fine dining along with their son Dan and wife Kathy. The Bibey's originally opened the restaurant with the simple principle of----"To serve good food in ample portions with superior service in a comfortable setting," and that principal still stands today.

While waiting to dine, relax on the waterfront gazebo with your favorite cocktail and listen to the music while enjoying the sunset. All the dinners are excellent which makes it really hard to say which is the most popular because there's so much to choose from on their menu. "Ok", so I will admit that I love seafood, therefore the option of creating my own seafood platter combination is just what the doctor ordered. You have a choice of 2 or 3 items which may include all the favorites such as shrimp, scallops, jumbo lump crabmeat, flounder, crab cakes, clam strips and the catch of the day. House specialties' include fresh flounder stuffed with crabmeat, broiled and topped with a lobster cream sherry sauce served with choice of starch and vegetable of the day. This is definitely a local's favorite. A loaf of fresh baked sourdough bread is served with most dinners. Desserts are also made fresh daily and include seven-layer cake, Key lime pie, peanut butter pie and others. They are all wonderful.

Enjoy live music on the waterfront gazebo deck in season. This is a great place to have a wedding and reception . Early bird specials are served from 4-5 p.m. Senior citizen discounts honored. For the little ones, there's a Little Whalers menu available. The Tale of the Whale restaurant is open from early spring to late fall serving dinner only. This is a very popular restaurant, so plan ahead.

Peanut Pie

Ingredients:
4 oz. cream cheese (softened)
1 cup confectioners' sugar (10X)
1/2 cup creamy peanut butter
1/2 cup milk
9 oz. whipped topping (cool ~whip)
1-9" graham cracker crust, baked and cooled
1/4 cup finely chopped salted peanuts

Optional ingredients for Chocolate Peanut Pie:
Oreo Cookie Pie Crust (instead of graham)
1/4 cup semi-sweet chocolate chips (melted)
   chocolate chips-crushed for topping

Directions:
1. Whip cream cheese until soft and fluffy
2. Beat in sugar and peanut butter
3. Slowly add milk, blending thoroughly into mixture
4. Fold Whipped topping into mixture and pour into pie shell
5. Sprinkle with chopped peanuts. Freeze until firm and serve.
   Can be re-frozen if not used.

For Chocolate Peanut Pie:
Proceed with steps 1-3. Add in melted chocolate chips.
Folds whipped topping in and pour into Oreo pie crust. Sprinkle with crushed chocolate chips.
Freeze until firm.

Top Dog Café

Highway 12
Waves, North Carolina

Joe & Pat Wolfe, Owners   (252) 987-1272

Top Dog Café was established in Waves in 1995 by Joe and Pat Wolfe, two "corporate refugees" who naively wanted to open up a "simple hot dog place" on Hatteras Island in order to escape the "big city rat race". The Café has since had to expand to survive, focusing more on burgers than dogs, adding wraps, salads, fish tacos, fried seafood, steamed seafood, pastas and so much more. The Wolfe's agree that they have aged considerably as the "rat race" now comes to them looking for good food while they are on vacation.

The café has expanded from just a mere, order your hot dog or hamburger and have a seat, to a rustic nautical theme restaurant that reminds one of the galley of an old pirate ship designed to reflect the personality of the island, its owners and staff. Check out the pirate and Jolly Roger flag in the crows nest.

The menu features huge, old-fashioned burgers (among other things) with an assortment of specialty toppings to tempt even the most discrimination taste buds. The burgers range in size from a 1-lb. "Big Kaboona" to a whopping 1 ½ lb. "Sunami." Those with huge appetites and a sense of adventure try the triple-decker "Sunami" version of the "Wild Thing or how about the 2 lb. Cyclone burger. The dinner menu features surf & turf, seafood baskets, oysters, crab cakes. Kids menu available. Beer and wine served.

"Wild Thing" Burger

½ lb. low-ft ground beef	¼ c. sliced jalapenos
1/3 c. chopped onions	½ c. grated Monterey Jack cheese
1 T. vegetable oil	

Sauté chopped onions in vegetable oil till softened. Cover, drain and place onions in a bowl to the side. Form ground beef into a patty and fry in pan over medium heat until browned on one side, then turn over and brown on other side till well done but still juicy. Cover pan and drain. Sprinkle grated Monterey Jack cheese over burger, cover pan and heat until cheese melts. Remove cover and top burger with sautéed onions and jalapenos. Serve on 5 inch seeded bun with lettuce and tomato, if desired. If a spicier "hot" taste is desired, jalapenos should be heated in pan for 1 minute before placing on burger to release additional "heat." Beware! Do not hover over pan as jalapenos are heated unless you want to clear your sinuses and burn your throat and eyes. The fumes are wild!

Tortugas' Lie

Shellfish Bar & Grill
P.O Box 1963, MP 11
Nags Head, North Carolina

Bob Sanders, Owner-Manager   (252) 441-7299
Richard Welch, Owner-Chef

Tortugas' Lie Restaurant has a growing reputation as being one of the areas' best moderately priced restaurants that continues to serve the most appetizing food on the Outer Banks. The menu features Caribbean inspired seafood, chicken, beef, and vegetarian dishes for lunch and dinner. Tortugas' also offers a full raw and steamed bar as well as specialty drinks, wine, buckets of beer and micro beers on the bottle or on tap. The chef's knowledge of spicy jerk seasoning and fruit-based sauces turns ordinary beef, chicken and seafood dishes into a culinary delight. In 2011, Coastal Living Magazine readers chose Tortugas' as one of "America's Top Favorite Seafood Dives".

Tortugas' has a very casual come-as-you-are type atmosphere which lends to its menu; there are even two beach volleyball courts right out back. You may order something as simple as a grilled fish burrito or hamburger right off the beach, or come in to dine on an entrée of grilled marinated mahi-mahi topped with a spicy pineapple salsa. So stop by to give them a try, and don't forget to take your volleyball.

Saint Martin Shrimp

1 lb. shrimp, peeled & deveined
2 c. coarse chopped tomatoes
1 lb. cooked fettuccine
1 small to medium red onion, julienne
4 T. minced fresh garlic
4 T. bacon, cooked & chopped
   (op. for veggies)
½ c. parmesan cheese, freshly grated

¼ c. chopped fresh parsley
½ c. dry white wine
Salt & pepper to taste
¼ c. olive oil
¼ c. butter

Sauté garlic and red onion in the olive oil until soft over medium to high heat. Add shrimp, stir, cook 1 minute, and add tomatoes, bacon, parsley, salt and pepper. Cook 1 minute and continue to stir. Deglaze pan with white wine and reduce liquid by one half by cooking down medium heat. Stir in pasta and butter over medium heat and cook until pasta is hot. Serve hot with fresh grated parmesan cheese. Serves 4.

Trio

Wine, Beer, Cheese

3708 N. Croatan Hwy, MP 4.5 Bypass
Kitty Hawk, North Carolina
www.OBXTrio.com   (252) 261-0277

Owners: Kenneth & Melissa Hyman,   John & Jennifer Minnich,

If you haven't been to Trio's you've definitely missed out on one of the most popular spots on the beach to meet with friends or just drop in for your favorite wine or beer. Trio's mission is to provide guests with an environment that is simple, elegant, and immediately comfortable. They're more than just a retail shop; just maybe a combination of an Italian Bistro meets English Pub.

Trio's is a combination of a retail wine shop, taphouse, bistro all rolled into one. Trio's has changed the way we think about wine here on the Outer Banks by offering a wine station dispensing system with 24 cellar condition wines that is self –service and available by the taste, half glass or full glass. It's a great way to explore the taste of expensive wines or just try one of the Old and New World producers for a few dollars. If beer is what you had in mind, then Trio Taphouse copper –top bar has one of the largest selections of rotating craft brews on the beach with over 24 beers on tap.

Kenneth and Melissa opened Native Wine in Point Harbor in 2003 to introduce interesting wines from around the world to anyone that would listen. With that said, business flourished and in 2011 they partnered with John and Jennifer to open "Trio" and the rest is history.

Trio specializes in hand-cut domestic and international cheeses with a selection of over 50 artisanal cheeses to stimulate your taste buds. There are always new cheeses to sample. A light menu featuring cheese & charcuterie plates, hot Panini, salads, dips, desserts are available. All of their dips, dressings, spreads and desserts are made in house.

Trio carries a huge selection of wines and beer from around the world in every price point from value quality to high– end and of course wines that you never even heard of. They offer a large selection of wines from 0–70% off.

Another great deal is the $10.99 and under selection of over 75 wines to choose from.

The mezzanine lounge on second level is perfect for private events, parties, gatherings. It's a great area to hang out with friends, play a little pool or just watch what's happening below.

No snobbish expectations here, just a cozy atmosphere, a menu of unique food options and a wide selection of wines from around the world. You're sure to discover a new favorite hang-out where the only expectations are to relax and be yourself. There simply is no better place to encounter good wine, good feelings and great company than Trio.

Stuffed Piquillo Peppers

Idiazabal is a firm, smoked sheep's milk cheese from Spain. It is available at better cheese retailers, or you may substitute any other firm, smoked cheese.

8 oz. Idiazabal, grated
2.5 oz. chorizo, cut into small dice
14 piquillo peppers
Balsamic vinegar, for drizzling
Heat oven to 350 degrees. In a small bowl combine the grated Idiazabal and diced chorizo. Fill each piquillo pepper with .75 ounces of the cheese mixture. Arrange peppers on a sheet pan and warm in the oven for 3-4 minutes until filling is warm and cheese is just beginning to melt. Transfer peppers to a serving platter and drizzle with balsamic vinegar. Serve warm.

Vilai Thai Kitchen
5230 N. Croatan Hwy. MP 1 Beach Rd.
Kitty Hawk, North Carolina

Vilai Hammock, Executive Chef, Owner   (252) 441-8424
Surasak (Mel) Hammock, Owner
Michael Hammock, Sous Chef, Owner

It's often said that good things come in small packages. Usually reserved for diamond rings and Mini Coopers, in this case it refers to Vilai Thai Kitchen. Vilai's is located in a small strip mall just across the street from the Hilton Hotel and next to the High Cotton Restaurant. Being a smaller location doesn't stop them from churning out top quality authentic Thai food either, as they offer take out and even catering options if you're not in the mood to go out. The restaurant atmosphere is relaxing with upscale Thai décor.

Chef Vilai moved from Thailand in 1980 and in 1987 started her career at the Sanderling Inn as a pastry chef and continued there until 2010. Her passion has always been to own her own restaurant. Her dream came true in 2010 when she opened Vilai Thai Kitchen. Together, Vilai and husband Surasak (Mel) designed and built the restaurant along with their son Michael. Michael, a great chef in his own right, has extended his culinary skills in crafting intricate and harmonious presentations of taste and flavor. You definitely might want to try Chef Michael's sushi as he prepares it every Saturday; his specialty is the "monster roll."

The menu offers appetizers, soups, salads, curries, noodle dishes as well as vegetarian dishes, fried rice selections and gluten free dishes; only the freshest ingredients are used in food preparation. For appetizers, try the spring rolls or the Thai style satay which is grilled on bamboo skewers and served with a side of peanut sauce and cucumber salad. Pad Thai is another favorite dish made with rice noodles in a spicy Thai sauce with your choice of meat, scallions, bean sprouts, egg, and topped with roasted peanuts.

Another favorite is the Thai Green Curry with coconut milk, Thai egg plant, peppers and scallions and your choice of meat or tofu and is served with a side of rice.

Don't forget to try one of Vilai's home made desserts. They are to die for especially the pecan pie and the peanut butter pie. Mango sticky rice is another favorite. Desserts change weekly.

Red and white wines are available along with Thai wines. Thai beer and many other beers are available. Open for lunch and dinner daily throughout the year. Catering is available.

Red Curry
Serving size -2

1 Tsp red curry paste
1 Tbsp sugar
1 Tsp salt
1 cup coconut milk
1 cup chicken stock
4 oz chicken breast

½ bell pepper
5-6 leaves of fresh Thai basil
2 oz. bamboo shoots
scallions

In hot pan --put coconut milk in sauté pan, bring to boil and add red curry paste, sugar and salt. Mix together, once all mixed, add chicken and chicken stock, let cook for five minutes then add basil, bell peppers, bamboo shoots, turn heat off and serve with steamed rice.

Weeping Radish Brewery & Restaurant

6810 Caratoke Hwy.
Jarvisburg, N.C.

Uli Bennewitz, Owner   www.weepingradish.com   (252) 491-5205
Torin Monro, Executive Chef   Jem Chapman, General Manager
Brew Master, Matt Glass   Season Tolson, Bartender

If you're heading for the Outer Banks, then you'll want to stop at the Weeping Radish Eco-Farm, Brewery, Restaurant and Butchery located just outside the town of Grandy in Currituck county. This well known restaurant and brewery was previously located in the town of Manteo but in 2006 moved the entire operation to its present location just 10 miles north of the Wright Memorial bridge. Uli wanted to expand his concept of all-natural beer to food with an Eco-farm with emphasis on raising fresh local products of meats, vegetables, produce and brewing beer the natural way. In 1986 Uli Bennewitz made history in North Carolina by opening up the first microbrewery in the state. The Black Radish beer was named one of fifty beers you should drink before you die. The brewery offers five year round beers and five seasonal beers for your enjoyment.

The farm restaurant gives the chef the opportunity to use the fresh meat, produce and brewery to offer the freshest ingredients of the day. The farm predicts what is offered on the menu of the day. Appetizers, soups, salads, burgers, sandwiches and German entrees offer a variety for everyone. The sausage sampler gives you a taste of their freshly make sausages. The bacon wrapped filet mignon with beer onions is another great menu item to try on the dinner menu along with the 12 oz. rib-eye. Children's menu available. Open year round. The ice skating rink will reopen again this fall and what a bit that has been.

Weeping Radish Bavarian Lambchops

8 lambchops
Chopped celery, onion, parsley, bay leaves (sautéed)
1 pt./1600 ml. Weeping Radish Springbock
2-3 onions thinly sliced

1 ½ lb./750g red potatoes, thinly sliced

Fresh chopped rosemary, and a little butter

Sauté lambchops in a little hot fat with the vegetables. Pour on the beer and lightly braise the chops for a few minutes. Strain off the liquor and put chops aside. Sauté onions very lightly until just soft, then layer with the potatoes to nearly fill a medium roasting dish. Pour over the beer liquid to reach just below the top layer. Top with a little butter and sprinkle with rosemary. Bake in a 375 degree oven for 45 minutes until the beer is almost absorbed and the potatoes tender. Place chops on top of potatoes and return to oven for about 10-15 minutes. Serves 4

To order additional copies of **Outer Banks Cuisine, A Sampling Of Our Restaurants with Recipes**, complete the information below

Ship to: (please print)

Name_____

Address_____

City, State, Zip_____

Day Phone_____

_____copies of Outer Banks Cuisine, A Sampling
Of Our Restaurants with Recipes @ $ 10.95 each $_____

Postage and handling @ $ 2.75 per book $_____

Enclosed is my check or money order for $_____

Make checks payable to and send to:

Dirt Enterprises
P.O. Box 262
Harbinger, North Carolina 27941
Phone (252) 491-2403
e-mail: beckysmithobx@yahoo.com

To order additional copies of **Outer Banks Cuisine, A Sampling Of Our Restaurants with Recipes**, complete the information below

Ship to: (please print)

Name_____

Address_____

City, State, Zip_____

Day Phone_____

_____copies of Outer Banks Cuisine, A Sampling
Of Our Restaurants with Recipes @ $ 10.95 each $_____

Postage and handling @ $ 2.75 per book $_____

Enclosed is my check or money order for $_____

Make checks payable to and send to:

Dirt Enterprises
P.O. Box 262
Harbinger, North Carolina 27941
Phone (252) 491-2403